"Ladies and gentlemen. Here [is the result] of event number nine, the one mile...

"First, number 41, R G Bannister of the Amateur Athletic Association and formerly of Exeter and Merton colleges, with a time which is a new meeting and track record, and which, subject to ratification, will be a new English native, British national, British all-comers, European, British Empire and world record.

"The time is three..."

Norris McWhirter

CONTENTS

CHAPTER 1:
Introduction

CHAPTER 2:
One moment in time

CHAPTER 3:
Milestones...
from Romans to
stagecoaches

CHAPTER 4:
Olympian efforts in a
professional era

CHAPTER 5:
Postwar... from
Finland to Sydney

CHAPTER 6:
Swede success

CHAPTER 7:
Doctor under orders...
and the three musketeers

CHAPTER 8:
This training
don't stop

CHAPTER 9:
He's behind you

Twenty years ago, many of the men who had held the mile record gathered at Oxford's Iffley Road track to celebrate Roger Bannister's achievement. Included in the line-up alongside Bannister are Arne Andersson, John Landy, Filbert Bayi, John Walker, Steve Cram, Noureddine Morceli, Derek Ibbotson, Herb Elliott and Michel Jazy.

FRONT COVER IMAGE:
A moment of sporting history – time stands still as Roger Bannister crosses the line in his world record attempt.

AUTHOR:
Tim Hartley

DESIGN:
Charlotte Pearson, Rosie Ward, Libby Fincham, Anita Waters

REPROGRAPHICS:
Jonathan Schofield and Simon Duncan

SENIOR SUB-EDITOR:
Dan Sharp

PRODUCTION MANAGER:
Craig Lamb

MARKETING MANAGER:
Charlotte Park

PUBLISHER:
Dan Savage

COMMERCIAL DIRECTOR:
Nigel Hole

PUBLISHED BY:
Mortons Media Group Ltd,
Media Centre,
Morton Way, Horncastle,
Lincolnshire LN9 6JR
Tel: 01507 529529

PRINTED BY:
William Gibbons and Sons,
Wolverhampton

WITH GRATEFUL THANKS TO:
Mervyn Benford,
Eamonn Coghlan, Peter Elliott,
Carol Haines, Richard Jones,
Matthew Fraser Moat,
Bob Phillips, Ray Webster.

All images courtesy of PA Images, unless otherwise stated. All images marked * are published under a creative commons licence. Full details at http://creativecommons.org/licenses

ISBN: 978-1-909128-40-8

All material copyright Mortons Media Limited, 2014. All rights reserved.

© Mortons Media Group Ltd. All rights reserved. No part of this publication may be produced or transmitted in any form or by any means, electronic or mechanical, including photocopying, recording, or any information retrieval system without prior permission in writing from the publisher.

CHAPTER 10:
After the event… how Bannister's life changed for ever

CHAPTER 11:
The race is over… but records tumble

CHAPTER 12:
African first, runner Walker… and the best of British

CHAPTER 13:
Out to Africa

CHAPTER 14:
An exclusive club

CHAPTER 15:
Women going hell for Leather

CHAPTER 16:
The last lap

CHAPTER 17:
Statistically speaking – facts and figures

INTRODUCTION

January 19, 2014, marked the end of an era, and the passing of a giant of British sport. It was announced that Sir Chris Chataway had died, and with the news came a host of black-and-white TV images and photographs... many of which focused on an event in which the remarkable Chataway – former government minister, first presenter of News at 10, world record holder and industry leader (his really was a Boy's Own life) – was 'best supporting player' rather than 'leading man'.

The images and commentary transported viewers back in time nearly six decades, to a very different world. But without Chataway and his contribution, well... who knows how the history of British sport would have panned out.

The TV schedules that January evening were full of the big money season opener of the new BBC dramatisation of The Musketeers, but for this writer in particular, thoughts kept drifting back to a very different band of three 'brothers', and this trio made real history. Chataway, Chris Brasher – a man who went on to a distinguished career in journalism and who co-founded the London Marathon, but who died aged 74 in 2003 – and Roger Bannister were the men who shook the sporting world as they quite literally passed a milestone many thought would never be reached.

Sixty years ago this year, May 6, 1954, to be precise, Brasher and Chataway helped propel Roger Bannister to become the first man to dip under one of sport's most enduring 'barriers'... the running of one imperial mile in less than four minutes.

What was so remarkable? Well, viewed from these modern days of synthetic tracks, computer-generated training regimes and sports science we may think nothing of attaining this strange 'old fashioned' distance in a time which seems fairly arbitrary, but back then, viewed in the context of a postwar world, it was stunning, uplifting, the attainment of a goal which had been just out of grasp for years, proving tantalisingly beyond numerous greats of the athletics world.

Words such as 'legend' and 'great' may be used with increasing frequency in 2014, devaluing the very worth of such phrases, but genuine stars of the athletics track had tried and failed to break the four minute barrier.

Men such as Walter George, John Paul Jones, Sydney Wooderson, Jack Lovelock and Gunder Haegg had all attempted it, had all come close, had all pushed the world record closer... but never quite done it. In fact there are many who believe Haegg and fellow Swede Arne Andersson could and should have done it were it not for the lack of competition during the war, as the neutral Swedes could have merely needed an international boost from British hero Wooderson and others to reach the athletics 'holy grail'.

And of course there have always been claims that runners had actually managed the feat years, perhaps many decades, before Bannister, but question marks over timing techniques, accurate distance measurement, and the fact that

athletics should be a sport for the gentleman amateur mean that the one time we can all be truly certain the barrier was breached was that windy day in Oxford just six decades ago. But still those rumours persist, and esteemed writers keep digging to establish the truth. I wish them luck in their quest, and await their publications with interest.

Just one year before Bannister, Brasher and Chataway set off on their record attempt, another great 'milestone' in human endeavour was reached, the scaling of Mount Everest by Edmund Hillary and Tenzing Norgay in May 1953. Since then more than 3000 people have stood where those men were once alone.

Last year the BBC reported how on just one day in 2012 more than 230 climbers reached the summit, forming an orderly

The first... (from left) Edmund Hillary, Colonel John Hunt and Sherpa Tenzing Norgay are pictured in 1953 after the successful expedition, led by Hunt, to Mount Everest. Remarkably more people have now stood at Everest's summit than have dipped under four minutes for the mile.

Record moment... Roger Bannister (centre) celebrates with Chris Brasher (left) and Chris Chataway in the aftermath of their record run in May 1954.

queue to get there and how Base Camp and nearby villages weren't quite the remote and wild destinations many might imagine, instead being heavily commercialised.

But this other peak, the magical running of a mile, four laps of a track in better than one minute per lap, has – according to respected journalist, author and statistician Bob Phillips, a man who maintains the definitive list of athletes who dip under four minutes for those 1760 yards – been reached by just over 1300 people.

So just consider for a moment… more people have stood on the 'roof of the world' than have emulated Bannister, and those greats who followed him. And this perhaps puts into context the difficulty of the feat, the gargantuan effort needed, the training, the discipline, the sheer willpower.

This publication will pay tribute to just some of the runners who got there and also to those who tried and failed. To those – like Brasher and the remarkable Chataway – who should never be 'bit part' players or 'supporting actors', but key figures in a truly remarkable story. We look at the talent of Sir Roger Bannister, and also look at how his record subsequently progressed.

How it has meant so much to so many… to men such as the great John Walker who held the record, and to those who never quite did, such as the kind and generous Eamonn Coghlan, who gave freely of his time and views, and the often-overlooked but very talented Peter Elliott – who shared his opinions on a great decade for Britain from the late 1970s onwards.

The recent passing of Chataway was a sad moment, a chapter closing on a great tale. There would no doubt have been plenty of focus on this remarkable man as the anniversary in May drew near, and it's such a shame that the first winner of the BBC's Sports Personality award is not here to enjoy the renewed adulation.

Many of these athletes have written books or had biographies on their remarkable careers published, so if this 'bookazine' does nothing more than inspire you to read further on these great characters then it will have been mission accomplished.

So without further ado… gentlemen and ladies, take your marks…

Tim Hartley, 2014

One moment in time

It was overcast, it was dull... it was, after all, England in early May. It had been raining, the wind was whipping through the university city of Oxford... on such days history is made.

After much agonising and soul searching, the record attempt was on, after all, who knew when John Landy or Wes Santee would try again to dip under four minutes for a mile run on a perfect track in perfect condition in Scandinavia or the United States? And if this chance wasn't taken...

In his book The First Four Minutes, Bannister said: "I had reached my peak physically and psychologically. There would never be another day like it." He hadn't raced since the previous August, everything was geared towards this attempt, and with Landy about to embark on a series of races in the homeland of Paavo Nurmi, it could be now or never.

The match between Oxford University and the Amateur Athletic Association had begun in squally conditions, but now, just in time for the start of the mile, the weather calmed. The flag on the top of the nearby church was released from the wind's grasp and six men lined up. Bob Phillips in his superb book The Quest for the four-minute mile, recalls how it should have been seven in the race, but... "the third member of the university team, medical student Nigel Miller, arrived straight from a lecture as a spectator, only to discover, when he read the programme, that he was due to run in the race. Frantic efforts to borrow kit failed and he missed the chance to be part of athletics' history".

The AAAs team in formation, but this was far more than just a race against the university, and Chris Brasher leads his colleagues Roger Bannister and Chris Chataway around the Ifley Road track, sticking to a strict schedule.

The six men – four representing the AAAs; Bannister, Chris Brasher, Chris Chataway and Derbyshire coal haulier (and Northern Counties mile champion) Tom Hulatt, plus two for the university; George Dole and Alan Gordon – were tense at the start, they knew what could potentially unfold, indeed Hulatt later told the *Derbyshire Times*: "Roger came up and said: 'don't hang on to me and Chris, we are going all out. You run your own race'."

Then... a false start, Brasher had gone too soon and was recalled by starter Ray Barkway, an Oxford athletics blue who died in a plane crash just two years later.

At the second time of asking they were under way and Brasher took the lead, with Bannister hot on his heels. In his book Bannister said: "I slipped in effortlessly behind him, feeling tremendously full of running."

Interviewed in 2000, he said: "I felt relatively calm, but of course (there was) quite a lot of adrenaline. I had to try to ensure the early pace was correct. I was a bit worried that he wasn't going fast enough, but I had done nothing for five days. I hadn't trained, I just rested, so I felt very full of running. I said 'faster, faster'. In fact, he was going absolutely the right pace."

Timings for that first lap vary depending which report you read, the *Guardian* favours 57.3, statistician and author Bob Phillips says 57.4, others say 57.5... but whatever, what's agreed is that Brasher's halfway pace was spot on: 1:58, and also that Brasher was 'running on fumes' and keen for Chataway to take over, which he duly did on the first bend of lap three. With Bannister right behind him Chataway led Bannister through three laps in a fraction over three minutes, just as Bannister wanted... he wanted to be delivered to this point with a fighting chance, and this was it... what would happen next would either create history, or be the latest in a long line of attempts which fell short.

Chataway later said: "That Roger could do it I didn't have the slightest doubt. The three-quarters was fine, but I was worried going around the next bend because I must have been slowing."

Then Bannister accelerated. As he memorably describes in his book, he said: "The moment of a lifetime had come. There was no pain, only a great unity of movement and aim. The world seemed to stand still."

In a later interview he recalled: "I knew that we were slowing down and I had to do the last lap in under 60 seconds... and that was quite fast. I overtook Chataway at the end of the last bend and then just had to run as fast as I could to the finish."

The scenes which followed went down in sporting history, Bannister crossed the line, mouth wide open, gasping for air, and collapsed into the arms of his friend the Olympic sprinter Nick Stacey – later a church minister – as people rushed on to the track, keen to know if sporting history had been made.

"I knew I was very close. I did collapse at the end, I think partly because if you don't keep on running, keep your blood circulating, then you get a kind of failure. The muscles stop pumping the blood back and you get dizzy. I did lose my sight for a bit because I was crowded in," Bannister later recalled. ➤

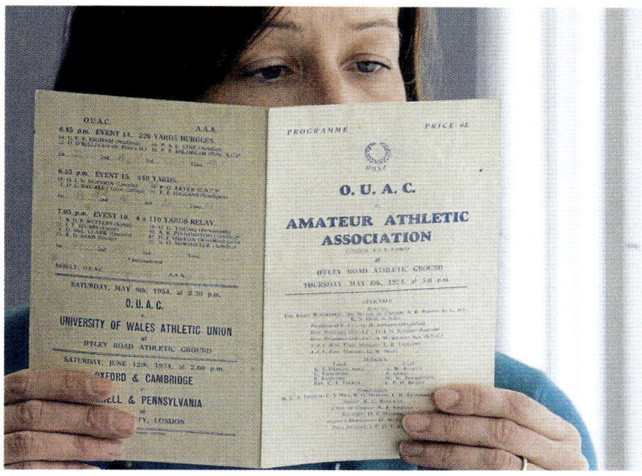

LEFT: A programme relating to the athletics meeting in 1954 went up for auction at a sports memorabilia sale in Scotland in 2008, being valued between £500 and £800.

FAR LEFT: The early stages, and a determined Chris Brasher sets a gruelling pace on the opening lap, a speed which would aim to give Roger Bannister a chance at the first sub-four mile.

BELOW: The final surge – Chris Chataway leads Roger Bannister into the final lap, 440 yards which would make history.

ABOVE: Stand by your watches – Roger Bannister just inches from the line, with a host of officials and supporters anxiously checking their timepieces.

FAR RIGHT: Exhaustion and delight, Roger Bannister in the immediate aftermath of the race, with coach Franz Stampfl, in his trademark flat cap, congratulating the new world record holder.

Chataway crossed the line second in 4:07.2, and Hulatt third in 4:16... but for the crowd, thought to be about 1200-1500 in number, the attention was now on timekeepers Harold Abrahams – the 1924 Olympic 100 metre champion – and Charlie Hill.

Both men's stopwatches said the same, and a note was passed to Norris McWhirter, the man who had the duty of announcing the result.

The loudspeakers crackled into life... and McWhirter began: "Ladies and gentlemen. Here is the result of event number nine, the one mile.

"First, number 41, R G Bannister of the Amateur Athletic Association and formerly of Exeter and Merton colleges, with a time which is a new meeting and track record, and which, subject to ratification, will be a new English native, British national, British all-comers, European, British Empire and world record.

"The time is three..."

The crowd erupted. The barrier had been broken. History had been made.

Pacemaking was frowned upon, but technically this had been a race, and the result was ratified. 3:59.4. A time which would go down in athletics folklore.

In his entertaining book 3:59.4 – The Quest to Break the 4 Minute Mile, John Bryant recalls a number of stories and events from later that evening, including how the Oxford Union interrupted proceedings by the proposal: "This house shall adjourn for three minutes 59.4 seconds," and also how Brasher, Chataway and Bannister were in central London that night – or technically, the early hours of the following day – when they asked a policeman directions to a nightclub. When he took his notebook out they feared they would be 'booked'... in fact, he asked for their autographs.

As George Dole, who came home in fifth place, later said: "I realised immediately that I had been part of an historic occasion."

On May 6, 1954 the sporting world changed for ever. A world record had been broken, and would be broken again very soon after in Scandinavia, but the quest was over. ■

The plaque placed in tribute to Derbyshire runner Tom Hulatt. Photo: Ray Webster, www.derbyshireheritage.co.uk

THE THIRD MAN

In a quiet corner of Derbyshire stands a tribute to the 'forgotten man' of the record-breaking race.

When people see that there were six athletes in the race between Oxford University and the AAAs, the assumption may be it was three for each team. However, there were four men representing the AAAs, Bannister, Brasher, Chataway... and Tom Hulatt. The man from Tibshelf was Northern Counties champion, and his presence made it a 'race' rather than an illegal pacemaking exercise.

A plaque commemorating Hulatt's part in the race stands on the Five Pits Trail at Pilsley, near Hulatt's home village, and the sign indicates that it's a mile from the plaque to Tibshelf. The former miner lived in the area until he died aged 59 in 1990.

Milestones...
from Romans to stagecoaches

What is it about the actual distance 'the mile' which captures the imagination or means so much... and who on earth would want to run one anyway? The mile is undoubtedly a massive part of British society and the English language is littered with references. Whether it's people talking at a 'mile a minute', cricketers hitting the ball 'a country mile', organisations reaching 'significant milestones' or their staff 'going the extra mile', millions of Britons – of all ages – refer to it in colloquial speech and expressions even when generations of youngsters have been brought up with metres and kilometres...

Miles are now viewed as 'old fashioned' thanks to metrication, which has been a strange phenomena in the UK – indeed for many nations. We're a mixed-up society which works in centimetres for some things, inches for others. Beer comes in pints, yet many of us buy our milk in litres then immediately approximate to pints. Petrol is now per litre... perhaps because it seems less expensive than gallons... and road signs are in miles. Basically we have every reason to be confused, have you ever tried explaining to youngsters how many pennies used to be in a pound...?

But the mile? Well, surely that's as British as they come, and there can be no quibble as to what it is, what it means and where it comes from. If that's what you thought, then perhaps it's time to think again, or at least in part, as the mile has a long and varied past.

Experts agree that the actual word originates with the Romans, and not only did all roads lead there, but every legion knew roughly how far away the mother city was. The soldiers measured their marches with the unit of distance mille passuum, which is generally translated as a thousand paces... but with each pace actually being two strides. After each 1000 paces a marker would be placed in the ground, but of course an army unit on a forced march might well have measured in a different way to a legion not rushing to quell restless natives. So the measure became standardised to an average pace length which historians estimate at 1479 metres or roughly 1618 yards.

In her book Marking the Miles: A History of English Milestones, Carol Haines acknowledged the Roman influence, and subsequent local variations, but as often seems to be the case when it comes to looking at sport and history, it was the British (or rather, the English) who decided what the rules should be.

"Many different measurements were subsequently used (following the Romans), but our 'statute mile' was first set down in a Parliamentary statute of 1593 to stop buildings being erected in London, Westminster, or three miles thereof," she wrote.

"It said that 'a mile shall contain eight furlongs, every furlong 40 poles, and every pole 16 foot and an halfe (sic)', i.e. 1760 yards. Several other mile measurements continued in use in Britain but in the 17th century the statute mile was adopted by the Post Office and by turnpike trusts. It was not until the Standard Weights and Measures Act of 1824 that the statute mile was established throughout the country."

Haines, a member of The Milestone Society – a group which aims to "identify, record, research, conserve and interpret for public benefit the milestones and other waymarkers of the British Isles" is fascinated with the way the measurement has become ingrained in our language and culture. ➤

> "Many different measurements were used, but our 'statute mile' was set down in 1593 to stop buildings being erected in London, Westminster, or three miles thereof"

OPPOSITE: It took more than 1000 years for Britons to build roads which compared to anything the ancient Romans left behind. This example of a Roman road in Ostia Antica, Italy, is still in use today.

BELOW: These images from the *Illustrated London News* in 1865 show the Notting Hill and Islington turnpike gates, both polygonal lodges located in the centre of the road.

This image from around 1830 shows the London coach approaching Magdalen Bridge into Oxford, ironically for this publication it's along what would now be Iffley Road (near where Bannister's mile was run). Experts suggest the coach would be doing about 10 miles per hour – i.e. a mile in six minutes... so not as fast as Bannister.

"If you put 'milestone' into (search engine) Google it will come up with hundreds of hits, but most will be of some significant event, such as milestones in medicine. So the measurement has made an impact with another meaning," Haines told the author.

"Although I am sure the EU would like us to convert to kilometres, I don't think many British people would willingly leave behind the mile, even though younger people may be happier these days working in smaller metric measurements."

About 9000 roadside markers, or 'milestones' are thought to still exist in Britain, but long before railways transformed transport these simple distance markers were everywhere.

But why should we care? Well the thing is, milestones were a vital tool, not only for knowing how far to a destination (like a medieval TomTom), but in commerce and revenue generation. The Romans may have built superb roads (and indeed buildings with tiled roofs, baths and many other features which few were able to replicate for a millennia), but of course that was the point... no one else did or could for many hundreds of years, and by medieval times these mud tracks which criss-crossed Britain became impassable as soon as weather turned nasty.

RIGHT: Before turnpikes, roads were rutted mud tracks. This 18th century engraving shows the Great North Road near Highgate on the approach to London. *

BELOW LEFT: The milestone on Oxford's Headington Hill – not part of the 'historic mile' highway system but a very readable example of its type on the present main road to London. Photo: Mervyn Benford

BELOW: This 1667 milestone on Morrell Avenue in Oxford is in far better condition than the one on Iffley Road... Photo: Mervyn Benford

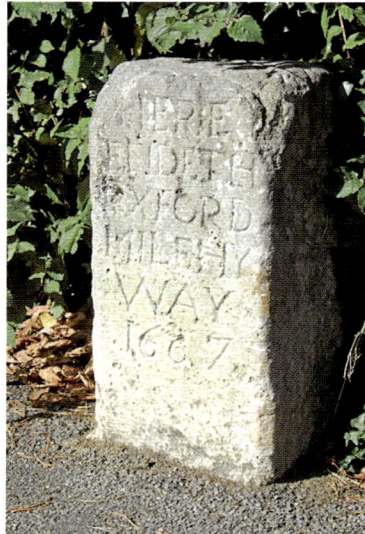

Frustration at the inertia of the transport system eventually led to the setting up of turnpike trusts, and under Acts of Parliament in the 18th and 19th centuries money was raised to build new roads... and charge users for travelling along them. Not popular with the general public.

The 'turnpike' name came from the spiked barrier at the toll gate, and from 1767 it became compulsory for mileposts to be in position on all turnpikes, not only to inform coach drivers and passengers of distance, but to help stagecoaches stick to their schedule... and for making sure the correct charge was applied when it came to changing horses at the next coaching inn. The distances were also used to work out postal charges before Britain introduced its uniform postal rate in 1840... and of course they were also very useful for measuring foot races.

So that's how and why Britain (or more precisely, England) used and developed the mile, but of course other nations had other ideas and there were many versions of the mile around the world. So for example the Arab mile used in medieval times was approximately 1925 metres, German-speaking states had miles equating to more than 7000 metres, similarly Denmark, while in Norway and Sweden distances for the 'mil' varied, sometimes between provinces of the same nation, but usually meaning a local mile was approximately 10 or 11 kilometres in today's measurements.

Of course, the British Isles is made up of more than just England, and the Scots' version was longer than the English mile, but as with many other nations, varied from district to district. It was eventually abolished in the Scottish Parliament and by the Act of Union, and was obsolete by the time the Weights and Measures Act of 1824 came into force, but in general, and allowing for those district variations, the Scots' mile was 1976.5 imperial yards, or just over 1.1 statute miles.

Ireland was different again, and due to the difference in length of the rod between the nations it meant the Irish mile was just under 2050 metres, or 1.27 statute miles. Such variances made life very difficult for mapmakers and engineers.

So the statute mile was set, yet what Britain can't claim as its own is the invention of running or races, they are as old as mankind. During the Industrial Revolution, when workers were in need of entertainment and when sports of all descriptions were blossoming and becoming formalised, the 'pedestrianism' of the 17th and 18th centuries was given new life. ➤

George Morland's painting The Turnpike Gate gives an idealised view of rural England.*

RIGHT: Manchester's Fallowfield Stadium was host to the FA Cup Final of 1893, a match in which Wolves beat Everton 1-0 in front of 45,000 people. It was the same venue at which Sydney Wooderson – see Chapter Five – set a world three-quarter mile record in 1939.

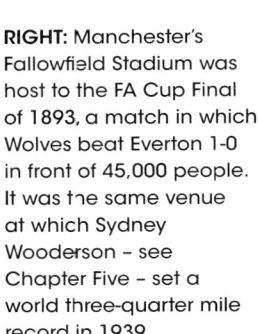

Pedestrianism was when aristocrats would wager on races between their footmen from one mile marker to another. In the 19th century it's no surprise that when a variety of Acts of Parliament gave workers rights and limited working hours, numerous sporting bodies and clubs were formed too.

Sports were codified, and helped bring a different clash into sharp focus... the drive towards professionalism versus the amateur ethos of sport, any sport.

The industrial north of England which included Derbyshire, Lancashire and much of the West Riding of Yorkshire, brought us football clubs and rugby clubs which are still in existence today, and at the same time the playing fields of private schools and the great universities were also developing their students' sporting excellence.

The factory workers were entitled to time off, so what could be better than using the afternoon to watch a game of association football, a game of rugby or an athletics event? The players or performers themselves? Well, they were finding it increasingly difficult to get time away from their work, so how could this be resolved?

Clubs which were attracting thousands of paying spectators could afford to make 'broken time' payments and reimburse sportsmen for taking time off work, and the logical extension was that they could become full-time.

However, the mainly upper and upper middle class people who tended to run sport were not keen on the existence of such professionalism, they felt it called into question the very ethos of sport, the 'Corinthian spirit'.

Thus in the final decade of the 19th century football allowed professionalism, and schisms appeared in rugby which led to the formation of the Northern Rugby Football Union and a split from the 'south', a split which eventually saw another game, rugby league, develop out of those common roots.

Athletics had seen the formation of the Amateur Athletics Association in 1880, but for years runners had been paid for their appearances at a wide variety of distances.

In his book 3.59.4: The Quest for the Four Minute Mile, the esteemed journalist and athletics commentator

BELOW: An artist's impression of an early floodlit match played at the Kennington Oval, circa 1878. The ground hosted football's first international match in 1870 between England and Scotland.

LEFT: Sport became far more organised in the late 19th century. Here the players and officials of Aston Villa's 1880 Birmingham Challenge Cup winning team of 1880 pose for the camera.

BELOW: This print, depicting a scene from circa 1810, shows the busy Surrey road Obelisk turnpike gate in London.*

Bob Phillips records how "gentlemen athletes and professional pedestrians raced against each other without any distinctions being made, and numerous well-attended matches took place", and says James Metcalf apparently won 1000 guineas when beating John Halton in a mile race of 1825. He adds that in 1841 a downhill mile was won in 4 mins 2 seconds in Kendal, Cumbria, for a stake of £500 and had allegedly been an attempt on 'the four minute barrier'.

But that was downhill, and advances in technology meant (relatively) accurate timing could be achieved. Tracks were a different matter, especially when it came to length and some circuits were just 200 yards, others more than 600. However, regardless of their length, what was key was the fact they were flat, well prepared and accurately measured.

So when it came to the mile, to records, and to achieving dreams, the stage was set... ■

Milestone Society members discuss the future of the Iffley Road 'Here endeth the Oxford Mile' highway stone of around 1640 with a local heritage officer. It was of course the Iffley Road track where Roger Bannister broke the four minute barrier in 1954.
Photos: Mervyn Benford

FOUR MINUTE MILE 17

Olympian efforts in a professional era
Taking to the track... and the amateurs are lagging behind.

Winning with style – one of athletics' great characters, Britain's Arnold Jackson, takes gold at the 1912 Olympics ahead of Americans Abel Kiviat (third left) and future mile record holder Norman Taber (746).

Athletics, like boxing, is rarely short of hyperbole, so when the 1912 Olympic 1500 metres final – the 'metric mile' – was described as featuring the greatest field of athletes yet assembled, it's something our cynical 21st century minds may well dismiss.

Indeed, through the 19th century there had been many 'greatest ever' races and challenge matches, but that 1912 race in Stockholm was significant for many reasons, not least of which is that the man who was to finish third, American runner Norman Taber, was to finally take athletics from the professional to the amateur era – a phrase which again, with our 21st century perspective, may seem incongruous. Taber finished just ahead of compatriot John Paul Jones, and both men were to enter the history books for their efforts over the mile.

But to understand the context, it's best to delve into the previous two centuries of athletics, pedestrianism, and record-setting… and some amazing characters who featured.

A sport which in Britain had started with races between the running footmen of the aristocracy soon became a lucrative betting opportunity for more than just the upper classes. The presence of milestones meant there were convenient markers on the turnpike roads, but in truth, any two landmarks would have served that purpose. The fact it was miles, and multiples thereof, simply provided a measure… and something the common man could relate to.

It's thought some mile races may have taken place as early as the mid 17th century, and journalist and author Bob Phillips believes there's good evidence of mile races in 1737, while he describes a race in 1787 in which Walpole, "a butcher from Newgate market", ran a mile ➤

FOUR MINUTE MILE 19

against a pedestrian named Pope, beating him in a time of 4:30. Phillips rightly has doubts over the actual time, but the principle of the competitive mile race was clearly established, as historian Peter Lovesey has plenty of anecdotal evidence from just before that Walpole race in which James Parrott is said to have run a mile along London's Old Street in four minutes.

One of the first to gain national prominence was Captain Robert Barclay Allardice (sometimes known as Allardyce), who had a remarkable range of racing distance and a training regime second to none, which author John Bryant describes as including running many times up a steep, grassy hill, rigidly controlled sleep patterns, the use of emetics and a high protein diet. A famous pedestrian, he covered 1000 miles in 1000 hours, the feature of these events being that rules stated you could only run one mile in any given hour, so it meant continuing 24 hours a day for several weeks. He was also an excellent runner, winning a mile race in 1804 in a time of 4:50, while he is recorded as having won a quarter mile race in 56 seconds.

A book published in 1813, Pedestrianism by Walter Thom, reported that a man called John Todd ran from Hyde Park Corner to the first milestone on Uxbridge Road in 4:10, and the training of such men was a serious business, as considerable sums of money were being wagered. So in such an entrepreneurial era it was never going to be long before promoters decided they could enclose tracks and charge spectators, as more and more people wanted to watch these races.

The sport therefore relocated from the turnpike roads and racecourses to purpose built stadia, often attached to public houses. Different parts of the country

Walter Slade, above, was one of the top amateur milers of the late 19th century and became a stockbroker in Australia.
Image: Illustrated Sporting News*

seemed to lay claim to different distance events, and it was northern cities which became a focal point for mile racing, with Manchester and Sheffield to the fore.

One of the first men to find national recognition and celebrity was Thomas Horspool, who was born sometime around 1830 in the Liverpool area. Horspool won the 1853 mile championship in Sheffield, then again the year after (in a recorded time of 4:29), and was champion miler for a third time in 1856, defeating John Saville.

The pair's biggest race came in September 1857 at what was to prove one of the UK's most important venues – Manchester's Copenhagen Sports Grounds. Established is 1857, the Copenhagen grounds became one of the country's leading sporting venues, hosting pedestrian events, wrestling, rabbit coursing and pigeon shooting, and all under the control of former professional runner Thomas Hayes.

He had seen what was happening – the fact that thousands wanted to watch sporting encounters and that there was money to be made – so he made sure that his venue was of top quality, the sort of place records could be broken and where the big professional names could attract big crowds.

Attached to The Shear's Inn, Newton Heath, the Copenhagen track consisted of a perfectly level and well drained 750 yard circuit, with a 235 yard straight. It was fully enclosed, "except where the canal forms a boundary", and crucially, there was a grandstand too.

Hayes attracted star names Horspool and Saville to race at his new venue in September of 1857, and it was Horspool who won by four yards, in the process matching Charles Westhall's five-year-old 'world record' of 4:28. Hayes declared the victor to be 'English ➤

"The 1912 Olympic 1500 metres final – the metric mile – was described as featuring the greatest field of athletes yet assembled."

LEFT: Walter George was a truly great athlete, and his 19th century records as a professional would stand into the second decade of the 20th century.

BELOW: The greatest race – the runners line up for the final of 1500 metres at the 1912 Olympics in Stockholm.

CITIUS, ALTIUS, FORTIUS…
THE IDEAL DISTANCE

The 1500 metres is often known as the 'metric mile'… but it's not quite a mile, and the Olympic Games, since its revival in 1896 by French aristocrat Baron Pierre de Coubertin, has featured a men's 1500m.

Many of those who have battled for medals in the Olympic games have been among the great milers of history, and many of those names will be discussed in later chapters… but the early games? Only die-hard fans would recognise some of the early medallists' names… yet they were often remarkable characters with great stories.

Characters include men such as Edwin (Teddy)  Flack (left), the English-born Australian who won the 1500 gold in Athens 1896, and also competed at tennis in those games, and the 1900 winner Charles Bennett, a train driver who was born in Dorset in 1870 and became known as the Shapwick Express.

Bennett was the first British athlete to win an Olympic gold medal. He died in 1948 and his grave was virtually forgotten until grandson Chris Bennett found it overgrown in the corner of a Dorset churchyard. A new headstone was donated by a Bournemouth stonemason in 2011, and now along with his granddaughter Chris tends the plot.

American Jim Lightbody won at the St Louis 1904 Olympics… against a fairly average field. However, it was 1908 when the top racers really started to take the event seriously, American Mel Sheppard (rejected by the New York Police Department on medical grounds) winning in London.

Four years later he was one of seven US runners who lost out to Britain's Arnold Jackson, one of those sporting characters who seems straight out of the pages on a novel. He had been an outstanding cricketer, footballer and boxer, and when he went up to Brasenose College, Oxford, he added oarsman and athlete to those sports he enjoyed. His training was 'casual' … but his performances were remarkable, winning the mile against Cambridge in 4:21⅘. In the 1912 Olympic final he entered the home straight in seventh place and overtook John Paul Jones, Abel Kiviat and Sheppard among others. His running career lasted for just half a dozen first-class races, and during the First World War he became the youngest brigadier-general in the British Army, was mentioned in despatches six times and won the DSO and three Bars.

Albert Hill has been mentioned elsewhere and he was an important figure in 20th century athletics both for his own efforts on the track, but also for his coaching. The Olympic champion in 1920, Hill beat fellow Briton Philip Noel-Baker (later Lord Noel-Baker) into second place at those Antwerp games – and Noel-Baker was another remarkable figure as the only man (so far) to have won an Olympic medal and received a Nobel prize (1959's Peace Prize).

Lon Myers (above) took on Walter George in a series of high-profile challenge matches.*

The first IAAF record holder John Paul Jones.*

Champion' at a time when there was no governing body, and he attracted Horspool back to his venue in 1858 where, on July 12, he lived up to his champion billing by defeating Manchester professional Job Smith in yet another record, this time clocking 4:23.

Not long after, Horspool retired from running. He was an undefeated champion and, as many others did, he became a publican, becoming landlord of a large public house near Nottingham.

Hayes needed new 'names' to fill the stands of the Copenhagen grounds, and he needed a new champion to take the boxing-style belt he had created to award the winner of the mile championship.

Step forward Siah Albison, and on October 27, 1860, he beat fellow young prodigy William 'Bill' Lang by just over a yard in 4:22¼ to retain the title he had won the previous August, and in a stunning world record. Albison, a weaver, was another who became a publican thanks to the profits of his running talent, and he was a central figure in a 'golden era' of athletics which saw a rivalry with Lang, and others, which was very much the (Seb) Coe, (Steve) Ovett and (Steve) Cram of its day. That 1860 championship race had also featured Jack White, Job Smith, and Charles Mower, and these men attracted thousands to the Copenhagen Sports Grounds as well as other major Manchester venues such as the City Grounds and the Royal Oak Grounds.

After losing to Mower, Albison regained his supremacy in a series of challenge matches, and ended his career with a record of seven wins from eight championship races.

Lang had lowered the record to 4:21¾ at the City Grounds in July 1863, while in April 1864 Londoner Teddy Mills smashed the record at the Royal Oak Grounds with a time of 4:20½, registering 60 seconds for the first lap, then throwing in a 68 second lap for the second 440 yards, the same again for the third lap, and increasing the pace to clinch the record.

It was an impressive mark, and was to remain the world's best for 16 months... before it was shattered in one of the greatest races of all time featuring the top men and perhaps including another 'first'... the presence of a pacemaker. On August 19, 1865, entrepreneur and promoter George Martin donated a cup for the winner of a mile race at the Royal Oak Grounds and all the champions of the era were there.

Included in the field of top professionals were Albison, record holder Mills, Lang, half mile record holder the Scotsman Robert McInstray, James Sanderson, Ireland's Patrick Stapleton, Welsh champion William Richards, plus pacemaker James Nuttall. Mills was forced to withdraw just before the start when he injured himself.

Nuttall did his job well, leading off with an opening 440 yards of 60 seconds, taking them through 880 yards in 2:05½ before Lang took it on. The final lap was reported as being fast and furious, with Lang attempting to pull away, McInstray keeping pace, and Richards hanging on for dear life, and in the final stretch Richards pulled level with Lang as McInstray faded... and the pair crossed the line with identical marks of 4:17¼, an amazing time... and one which would stand for 16 years. A decider was held a week later, with Lang beating Richards in a time that was a full five seconds slower.

The next man to lower the record was a phenomenon from Paisley in Scotland, 'Young Willie' Cummings. Born in 1858, he was a professional runner by the age of 18, and as early as 1877 he had run a mile in the more than respectable time of 4:28½, and lowered his best to 4:25 the following year.

While still only 20 he ran the fastest mile in Scotland, 4:18¼ in September 1878, and followed that up within two weeks by posting a time of 4:19½. He was clearly the top man, descriptions from the time and soon after portray him as standing just 5ft 6in and weighing a mere 8st 10lb, while journalist Bob Phillips quotes David A Jamieson describing Cummings as "one of the prettiest runners who ever put on a running pump".

> "Young Willie Cummings, a professional by the age of 18, was described as 'one of the prettiest runners who ever put on a running pump.'"

In May 1881, and in pouring rain at Preston, Cummings took on William Duddle – one of the few men who seemed capable of pushing 'Little Willie' – and finally lowered that long-standing world record of Richards and Lang, taking it down to 4:16½.

But like many sports were to find over the coming decades, a dominant force sometimes made things predictable, and the thrill of sport was the unpredictability, the uncertain outcome. For a sport which attracted such heavy betting this was a problem, and the seemingly invincible Cummings was becoming a victim of his own success, the crowds were falling and interest waning as there seemed little competition in the professional ranks for such a towering force as the diminutive Scotsman.

However, there was an amateur who was making waves and might just have the ability to defeat the champion – Walter George. Could the amateurs be about to take over? Actually, no, we still have to wait until the second decade of the 20th century for that, but George had certainly closed the gap, and surely the best ought to meet the best?

The Amateur Athletic Association was formed in July 1880 and George, who was winning virtually every title possible at a large range of distances, petitioned the

governing body to be allowed to face the professional champion Cummings, but to no avail.

Born in 1858, by the age of 16 George had been apprenticed to a chemist and as with many people, worked long hours. His weekends were his chance to exercise, and he took up cycling and walking races. It's said that by the age of 20 he had told friends that he was capable of running a mile in 4:12, and mapped out a way of doing it, knowing the 'split' times he would need. He was certainly ambitious, because at this time in 1878 the amateur world best was 4:24½ while the professional best was the seemingly unassailable 4:17¼. His theory was that quarter-mile splits of 59 seconds, 2:02 and 3:08 would see him to that ambitious 4:12.

He won the mile event at 1879's Amateur Championships of England in a time of 4:29, and the following year, in the inaugural AAA championship, again took the mile in a time of 4:28⅗. On August 16 of 1880, London's Stamford Bridge saw him in a race which promised much, his first quarter's split being his 'ideal' 59 seconds, however, he fell away to finish in 4:23⅕, a new amateur world record, but outside his declared target of 4:12.

George went from strength to strength. He ran 4:19⅖ on June 3, 1882, and by now only three men had ever run faster, all of those being professional. The George bandwagon crossed the Atlantic and he faced top US miler Lon Myers in a series of races in November.

The event was phenomenally popular, and an estimated 130,000 people paid to watch the three races – of varying distances – at New York's Polo Grounds. The first, a half-mile clash, saw Myers beat George 1:56⅗ to 1:57, while the following week the Briton prevailed in the mile race, recording a time of 4:21⅖ to the American's 4:27⅗. It all came down to the three-quarter mile race, and 60,000 spectators saw the local hero record a time of 3:13... finishing second to George's 3:10½.

The following year, 1883, George was taken ill and was unable to defend his AAA mile title, although he did recover to win the 10 mile event and break his own record, then the following year he reclaimed the AAA mile championship, defeating defending champion William Snook in a race at Birmingham, finishing in 4:18⅖... yet another amateur record time.

The fact that in that same year he took the amateur half-mile, four miles and 10 mile titles, plus the cross-country, and set world best marks at a host of other distances, merely emphasised his dominance.

ABOVE AND BELOW: The opening ceremony at the Panathinaiko stadium in Athens, and a programme from the second games in Paris.

PROGRAMME

DES

JEUX OLYMPIQUES DE 1900

PARIS

Comité International des Jeux Olympiques:

Président. M. le Baron PIERRE DE COUBERTIN

Comité d'Organisation des Jeux Olympiques de 1900

Programme des Jeux

ABOVE AND ABOVE RIGHT: American James Lightbody took gold in the 800 metres and 1500 metres at the St Louis games of 1904.

But of course he wasn't quite the very best in the world... and if he raced 'Willie' Cummings then he would lose his amateur status.

Finally, by 1885, George decided the professional route was for him – perhaps because of mounting debts, perhaps purely for the sporting challenge, so a match, or series of matches between the two men, was set, with the first being on August 31, 1885, at Lillie Bridge in south-west London, a site now occupied by Earls Court.

In scenes which would be repeated in the first ever Wembley FA Cup final, a massive crowd wanted to be there, and the organisers were overwhelmed. More than 30,000 people turned up, and crowds angry that they had been locked out forced their way in and completely encircled the running track "both inside and out". It's thought that the barricades to the venue were broken down when the starter tested his pistol, and hearing the gunshot the thousands still outside rushed through.

The race itself, as with many two-man races, was perhaps an anticlimax, as the first quarter mile was reached in 58⅗, the half mile in 2:01 and the three-quarter distance in a fraction over 3:07, but in the final 440 yards George pulled away and Cummings eased off, already beaten, to finish almost 70 yards back as the winner recorded a time of 4:20⅕. It's reported that George himself eased back significantly, so the time could have been a lot faster.

The two had signed up for a three-match series, and Cummings easily won the other two races, one being a four mile race at Powderhall in Edinburgh, while the final clash was a 10 mile encounter again at Lillie Bridge.

It was the mile which was the glamour race though, and it's understood that in trials and practise events just weeks before his professional debut, George ran a 4:14½, then, even more impressively, he took part in a handicap race and recorded splits of 58⅕, 1:58⅗ and 3:07. The winning time of 4:10⅕ for a race which wasn't sanctioned and therefore not 'official' was simply beyond belief, so the track was remeasured and it was found he had run six yards too far. All of which backs up the thought that the 'easing up' race could have seen a much better time recorded.

George was clearly in remarkable form and this was proving to be a serious rivalry. The pair's most famous encounter occurred in 1886, in a rematch of their mile challenge from the year before. On August 23, again at Lillie Bridge, the two men attracted another large crowd, this time consisting of 20,000 spectators.

The starting gun was fired by former two-mile record-holder Jack White and George led from the off. The first 440 yards was passed in 58¼, and Cummings was hot on his heels and looking relaxed. At the half mile, George went through in 2:01¾, a very strong pace, and it was clear this was a serious contest.

They passed the three-quarter mark in 3:07¾, and Cummings made his move, pulling level before kicking for home with 350 yards to go.

BELOW: Glorious London... the White City Stadium, venue for the 1908 Olympic Games.

LEFT: 1904 Olympic champion James Lightbody crosses the line to claim gold.

George held his nerve and his form, and closed the gap again before pulling ahead. Cummings collapsed and George crossed the line after an epic duel.

The time was all-important, and when it was chalked onto the blackboard there was a roar from the crowd, the world best had been shattered, lowered to 4:12¾. Cummings had lost the race and the record, and when it came to that world best mark, George would be king for nearly three decades.

Cummings took a measure of revenge by defeating George in a four mile challenge, but George won a 10 mile clash easily. In 1888, the Scotsman defeated George in a three-quarter mile race plus two one mile races, though the times never reached those heady marks of 1886...

Of course there were still world records for amateurs, and the top man in this period was Thomas Conneff, an Irishman who emigrated to the US at the end of the 1880s, and who by the start of the following decade was emerging as the best of the amateur milers.

On August 26, 1893, he beat Walter George's amateur best time (George still held the overall time of course, now as a professional), when setting a time of 4:17⅘ in a race at Cambridge, Massachusetts, and with a first lap of 59 seconds and a 880 yard time of 2:00 he was a serious threat to the record books.

Conneff's record lasted almost two years before Frederick Bacon recorded a time of 4:17 at the AAA Championships at London's Stamford Bridge on July 6, 1895, and this inspired the US-based Irishman to attempt to regain his world best.

At Travers Island, New York, barely six weeks after Bacon's best, Conneff was paced to a first 440 at 62⅖ seconds, the half mile in 2:06⅗ and the three-quarter mark at 3:10⅘. With renewed effort he stopped the watch at 4:15⅗ to claim back his amateur mile world best. Just a few weeks later, on September 21, he beat the best amateur milers that Britain had to offer in a time of 4:18⅕.

The respected reporter William B Curtis – himself a champion athlete, and who was a founder of the New York Athletic Club in 1868 – is reported to have said of Conneff: "He never was in such fine mettle as during the past four weeks. He could at any time have beaten his own world's best amateur record of 4:15⅗ and might have equalled or surpassed the world's best professional record, 4:12¾. He is one of those athletes who speedily makes their handlers go gray-haired (sic), is restive ➤

BELOW: Canada's John Tait was one of those who lined up in the 1908 1500 metres final.

THE ENEMY WITHIN? ATHLETICS' AMATEUR MOVE

The name Walter George will doubtless crop up again and again in this publication, with various adjectives attached such as 'great', 'innovative' and 'record-breaking'... plus two other words which will feature heavily – 'amateur' and 'professional'.

George was the amateur world record holder, but he wasn't the best miler until he beat 'Young Willie' Cummings, and for this – as mentioned elsewhere in this chapter – he'd have to turn professional.

In the 21st century the whiff of corruption can occasionally hang around sport, as betting syndicates across the world wager on the outcomes of events, or even what happens at various stages within events, and in 19th century athletics it was no different. Once a professional George was the best at what he did, he was running for prize money and records, he had no need to go a bit slower in order to help a bookmaker, but pedestrianism was really driven by gambling and paying spectators who flocked to those new tracks. Below those elite challenge matches it became notorious for corruption as athletes were frequently in league with bookmakers.

The middle and upper classes who dominated the establishment had a clear self-interest in blocking the professionalisation of sport... as this made it feasible for the working classes to compete against them with success.

Meanwhile, the growth of public school and university sport gave rise to a number of new clubs, and the Amateur Athletic Club was formed in 1866 by John Graham Chambers, a Cambridge man, with the aim of 'controlling' the sport in the same way the MCC (Marylebone Cricket Club) oversaw the laws of cricket, and making sure the 'spirit' of sport remained intact. The London Athletic Club was soon founded as a rival to this, while northern clubs formed their own association... the situation was rapidly becoming a mess.

On April 24, 1880 the Amateur Athletic Association (AAA) was founded at the Randolph Hotel, Oxford at a meeting arranged by three Oxford University athletes: Clement Jackson (uncle of Arnold Jackson, the 1912 Olympic 1500 metre champion), the Australian Bernhard Ringrose Wise and Montague Shearman. Invitations were sent to the country's leading athletic clubs, and the aim was to resolve the ongoing power struggles.

A key part of the negotiations was the use of the term 'amateur', some argued it meant a 'gentleman' by birth, others that it was simply anyone who did not compete for money. After much discussion it was eventually decided the new Oxford definition would be: "one who has never competed for a money prize or staked bet, or with or against a professional for any prize, or who has never taught, pursued or assisted in the practice of athletic exercises as a means of obtaining a livelihood".

As many would find to their cost, such a definition would eventually exclude some greats of sport, and once Walter George's record was eventually broken by Norman Taber, the mile record would become an amateur preserve for generations.

ABOVE: The crowds flocked to the White City Stadium during the 1908 London games.

under the restrictions of training, and prone to stray outside the bounds laid down for athletic aspirants. He is now 29 years old and can hardly hope to improve hereafter."

The next man to lower the amateur best, and who helped link the eras of the professional, amateur and Olympian, wasn't even born when Walter George set his world best mark in London.

John Paul Jones, who was born in October 1890, will always go down in history as the man who held the first mile record to be ratified by the International Amateur Athletics Federation in 1913, while two years earlier he had lowered the amateur best mark too.

A popular all-round sportsman, when he entered Cornell University he didn't really consider himself an athlete, but under coach Jack Moakley he enjoyed plenty of cross country success.

That first entry into the record books came on May 27, 1911, at the Soldiers Field stadium in Allston, Massachusetts. Against strong opposition he won by 10 yards in a time of 4:15⅖, a new amateur world record. But he was running for the team too, and later that day won the 880 yards to give Cornell the IC4A championship.

Jones wasn't keen on the long trip to Sweden for the 1912 Olympic Games, but was persuaded to enter and be part of that 'greatest field of athletes yet assembled'.

Also running were 1908 Olympic champion Mel Sheppard, Britain's Arnold Jackson (who later became Strode-Jackson), plus Norman Taber from Providence, Rhode Island. Fellow US athlete Abel Kiviat, who held the 1500 metre world record, was heavily favoured, but it was Jackson (who later became a brigadier general) who won gold, ahead of Kiviat, Taber and Jones in fourth. Jackson was a remarkable character in his own right. He took up running (he had been a rower) just the year before, and Stockholm was the first time he had run anticlockwise around a track, as English races were usually clockwise.

Back in the States the following year Jones ran an indoor mile in 4:19⅘, then on May 31 in a race at Cambridge, Massachusetts, he beat Taber to win in a time of 4:14⅖ (or 4:14.4)... a new amateur record and the first mile record to be recognised by the new governing body of track and field, the IAAF (and the mark at which for the purposes of this publication, we go from fractions to decimal... a new era deserves a new system). Soon after Jones graduated... and then retired from the sport.

LEFT: Mel Sheppard, gold medal winner in the 1500 metres in 1908.

RIGHT: Sheppard crosses the line ahead of Great Britain's Harold Wilson.

Whether he would have gone on to greater successes will always be open to debate, but what is undeniable is that the next man to step up finally laid the ghost of Walter George to rest, and became the first amateur to surpass that 30 year hoodoo.

Norman Taber, who was born in September 1891, made the breakthrough to the top ranks in 1910 when finishing third in the IC4A (Intercollegiate Association of Amateur Athletes of America) championship mile for Brown University. He was selected for the 1912 US Olympic team and battled with fellow countryman Kiviat for the lead in the 1500m before both were overtaken by Britain's Arnold Jackson.

Back home his second place in that race, which saw Jones recognised as the IAAF record holder, placed him fourth in the all-time amateur ranks and he continued to race and record impressive times.

As the rest of the world went to war (the US would not formally enter the conflict until 1917) athletics continued in the United States, and Taber was in the form of his life in 1915 after training with coach Eddie O'Connor. On June 26 he beat Kiviat, recording a time of 4:15.2, then a few weeks later he won another mile in 4:17.6... so he was in the shape to do it, but he was not just after Jones' IAAF best.

On July 16 the Harvard track at Allston, Massachusetts, was the perfect venue, and pacemakers were in place. He recorded 58 seconds for the first lap, the half-mile was reached in 2:05, the three-quarter stage in 3:13... then as the finish line loomed it was down to Taber. He went past the 1500m mark in an unofficial 3:55, faster than that world record, and finally reached the mile in 4:12.6.

After 29 years someone had finally eclipsed George's time. While many died on the battlefields of Europe, including a number of Olympic medalists such as Britain's Harold Wilson, the 1908 1500m silver medal winner who had turned professional in 1909, triple AAA champion George Butterfield and 1914 AAA mile winner George Hutson, the record had gone... just... ∎

Stockholm celebrated hosting the 1912 games.

The teams lined up for the opening ceremony of the Stockholm Olympics.

THE OLYMPIC DREAM

The modern Olympics – as any sports fan will know – began in 1896, and Athens was chosen as the host city.

Pierre de Coubertin, whose idea an Olympic revival was, had espoused the idea in an article he wrote in 1890, and had been inspired by a sporting event which had been founded four decades earlier in the English village of Much Wenlock. But there were several other sporting festivals right across Europe which were named after the Olympic games in Ancient Greece.

De Coubertin called a congress at the Sorbonne in Paris in 1894 to present his plans for an Olympic revival to representatives of sports from 11 nations, and his idea had been for the new event to coincide with the Paris Exposition of 1900. However, six years was a long time away and 1896 was decided upon instead… and eventually Athens settled upon as a venue, not least because of those Ancient Olympic roots. Coubertin was a fan of the amateur ethos, of the ideals of sport, so professional competitors were excluded.

However, controversy was never far away, even in the days of those early games. One of the most famous examples of the Olympic 'inflexibility' was the case of American Jim Thorpe. He had his gold medals in the decathlon and pentathlon from the 1912 Olympics stripped, and his achievements removed from the record books, because he had once accepted small amounts of money for playing semi-professional baseball during his college summers.

Thorpe went on to have a distinguished career in American Football and those Olympic medals were eventually reinstated in 1983, three decades after Thorpe's death, on compassionate grounds.

One of the most staunch defenders of the Olympics' amateur ethos was the International Olympic Committee's president from 1952 to 1972, the American, Avery Brundage. In a 1955 speech, he said: "We can only rely on the support of those who believe in the principles of fair play and sportsmanship embodied in the amateur code in our efforts to prevent the Games from being used by individuals, organisations or nations for ulterior motives."

Roger Bannister may have been the very 'ideal' of an Olympics competitor, a world class athlete in student and post-grad days who then went on to a full career, but some nations had other ideas, and Eastern Bloc countries would have athletes who held positions in the armed forces or other jobs specially created for them and yet which meant they were effectively full-time competitors.

After the 1988 games in South Korea, the IOC decided to make professional athletes eligible for the Olympics, subject to the approval of the various international federations.

Top-class mile running was one of those events which seemed to have gone full circle, from the days when the professional Walter George was dominant, through the amateur era, and back to professionalism. ■

RIGHT: A commemorative torch at Linden Field in the village of Much Wenlock marks the birthplace of the Olympics.

FAR RIGHT: America's Jim Thorpe was one of the most high profile early victims of professionalism.

BELOW: Panathinaiko Stadium (also known as the Kallimarmaro or the ancient marble stadium) also hosted events at the 2004 Olympics.

Postwar...
from Finland to Sydney

A forgotten great of British middle-distance running, Albert Hill did the 800 metres and 1500 metres 'double' at the Antwerp Olympics of 1920, when many considered him too old. He would go on to influence later generations through his coaching.

The First World War claimed the lives of millions, and among them were some of the finest athletes of the day, and doubtless many who would and could have emerged to claim records and glory.

As would happen nearly three decades later, athletics continued through the war years, and neutral nations saw some impressive performances, most notably Sweden and the US.

Norman Taber took the world mile record during the war years, finally lowering Walter George's mark, while across in northern Europe, the Swede John Zander was burning up the track in the 1500 metres, recording a time of 3.54.7 at Stockholm's Olympic Stadium in 1917, and lowering Abel Kiviat's world best time in that event. It was the equivalent of a time just outside George's best for the mile, and a year later he crossed the line in 4:16.8, making him the first non-English speaking athlete in the top 10 mile rankings.

The immediate postwar years were difficult as the world readjusted, and one of the leading athletes of the time provides one of those direct links through sport and history which takes us from the great Chariots of Fire coach Sam Mussabini through to Roger Bannister. Londoner Albert Hill had enjoyed success in the four mile race at the AAAs in 1910, and once he joined the Polytechnic Harriers he was coached by Mussabini.

After serving for most of the conflict in the Royal Flying Corps, the railway worker was demobbed in 1919, just in time to get back into training and prepare for the 1920 Olympics in Antwerp. But at the age of 30 many considered him too old for the games... something he proved was plainly ridiculous by claiming both the 880 yard and one mile titles at the 1919 AAA Championships, then going on to equal the British record for that latter distance at 4:16.8. ➤

In Antwerp he again did the 'double' of 800 and 1500 metres – a feat which no Briton would repeat until Kelly Holmes in 2004, and the following year won the AAA mile in 4:13.8, just over a second outside the world best, and remarkable for a man who had been fighting for his country during his 'peak' years. Hill retired from running and became a coach... and will feature again in the quest for the sub-four minute mile.

But the world record remained stubbornly intact... until a new decade and a new era dawned, and that era had a name... Nurmi.

It's the mark of real fame or reverence when just one name will suffice for people to know exactly who you mean. It happens quite often in sport – Pele, Eusebio, Ali, and showbusiness is rife with it, but in the 1920s athletics was dominated by one man, Paavo Nurmi – a phenomenon from Finland, and who became the greatest of the 'Flying Finns'.

Born in the port of Turku in June 1897, Nurmi bestrode the sport and won gold at the 1920, 1924 and 1928 Olympics, and experts say he never even took the mile seriously, as his range of distance was so great he never truly concentrated on the event and pushed it to his limit.

During Nurmi's peak years he was unbeaten at distances from 800 metres upwards for 121 races, while he was never beaten at the 10,000 metres or cross-country. He won nine Olympic golds in total, and as writer John Bryant says: "He set so many world records that statisticians still argue over the number."

It's always said that the working class Nurmi had been inspired by the efforts of compatriot Hannes Kolehmainen, who won gold at the 1912 Olympics and at a time when Finnish nationalism was a hot topic – his victory in Stockholm saw the Russian flag raised, as Finland was a state in the Russian empire.

But even before then he was showing immense promise, and the young Nurmi was an active child, and eldest of five. He and his friends would run or walk several miles each day, and even before that Olympic inspiration of Stockholm he was keen on athletics, hanging around the track in Turku. When only aged 11 it's claimed he begged athlete Fabian Liesinen to put a stopwatch on his efforts over 1500 metres… and the resulting time of 5:02 was sensational.

The son of a carpenter, Paavo Nurmi's life changed forever when his father died in 1910 and he was forced to become the main breadwinner to help the family, working as an errand boy for a wholesaler… but even this kept him fit, as he spent hours every day pushing the delivery cart. However, inspired by Kolehmainen's efforts he returned to running, with cross country featuring heavily – both running and skiing.

His training techniques were doubtless influenced by this active outdoor lifestyle and included walking, sprints and calisthenics, but it was during his national service when he came to prominence as an athlete, and where his legendary iron discipline came to the fore. It's said that while others marched with backpacks and rifles, Nurmi ran; that rather than train in running shoes, the heavy army boots helped strengthen his legs… and even that he ran behind trains and trucks, holding the rear of the vehicle, as it helped to lengthen his stride pattern. This would make perfect sense to Nurmi though, because back home in Turku he had run alongside the trams to pace himself, perhaps the first (and youngest) example of an athlete using mechanical training aids?

He was an innovator in the extreme and obsessed with the detail of training. It's understood he became vegetarian, he didn't touch coffee, tea, tobacco or alcohol, and he always liked to learn from his mistakes – or what he perceived as mistakes. His first race in the 1920 Antwerp Olympics was the 5000 metres, and leading from the start he was eventually passed by Frenchman Joseph Guillemot (the only time he was ever beaten by a non-Finn in the Olympics) to come home in silver medal position.

> "Nurmi became vegetarian, didn't touch coffee, tea, tobacco or alcohol, and he always liked to learn from what he perceived as his mistakes."

BELOW: Finnish dominance – Sweden's Finnish-born Edvin Wide leads the 'real' Finns Ville Ritola and 'Peerless Paavo' Nurmi around the Olympic track in 1924, a games at which Nurmi would win five golds.

The Frenchman was another remarkable character, his heart was on the wrong side of his chest and he had almost died from gas poisoning during the First World War. As the French athlete congratulated Nurmi he vomited on the Finn's spikes, so great had been his exertions.

Nurmi took revenge on the same opponent in the 10,000 metres and also took gold in the cross country individual and team events. But although we are still not discussing the mile, this is a significant period, as the defeat to Guillemot prompted more Nurmi analysis, his theory being that a more even pace would be better than a fast start. Thus the Finn took to running while holding a stopwatch, and in many images of that time you will see him consulting the watch and oblivious to opponents and the crowd.

This became a golden period for Nurmi, and over the next few years he expanded his training… and his fame, and it's at this point that he took the mile world record in Stockholm in 1923, but it was never his main distance – 10,000 metres always being the one closest to his heart.

His first world record at that distance was also set in Stockholm, in 1921 and the following year he beat the world best marks for the 2000m, the 3000m and the 5000m, while in the same year as he took the mile record down to 4:10.4 – a massive 2.2 seconds off Taber's official best mark – he also secured the 1500m world record, then for good measure he added the 1923 national 800 metres title. ➤

ABOVE: With the young Paavo Nurmi concentrating on longer distances at the 1920 Olympics in Antwerp, Britain's Albert Hill (398) took gold in the 1500 and 800 metres.

BELOW, AND RIGHT: Four years later in France and 1924 Olympic 1500m gold medal winner Paavo Nurmi (second left), gets set for the off in the final.

The mile record is one many believe Nurmi could have lowered even further if he had concentrated fully upon it. He believed he could used his mastery of even pace running to produce four 62 second laps and a time of 4:08. He prepared for that 1923 Stockholm race in true Nurmi style – the track for what would be a challenge between Nurmi and the Finnish-born Swede Edvin Wide was 385 yards, so he reproduced those dimensions back in Finland. In the race itself the first 440 yards was faster than Nurmi had wanted, 60.1 seconds, and at the three-quarter mark they had recorded 3:06.7. For the final 440 he was relentless and won by nearly 20 yards in that world record of 4:10.4. But after that, despite many now being convinced that the four minute barrier was within reach, and 'Peerless Paavo' could do it with his even pace mastery, he concentrated his running efforts elsewhere.

Nurmi is of course a fascinating and complex character and worthy of books in his own right, and while the story of the mile features him as one of the record breakers, it was also for his training methods and 'professional attitude' that he demands inclusion in any story of the mile as a race and event.

His story continues mainly at longer distances, but his efforts at the Paris Olympics of 1924 bear mention, as by this stage he was the dominant figure in world athletics, and a superstar back in Finland. There had been fears for his participation earlier that year due to a knee injury, but he recovered in time to resume his gruelling twice-a-day training regime. The organisers at Paris had scheduled the 1500 metres and 5000 metres within an hour-and-a-quarter of each other, but Nurmi, ever the man for preparation, was ready for this, having earlier that year run both distances within an hour of each other… setting a world record in each.

Come Paris and he won both events with just a light massage and a snooze in-between races, although the 5000 saw athletes trying to 'burn him off' early in the belief he must be tired… but to no avail. The next day, in the Paris heatwave, he won the 10,000 metres cross country gold in an event which saw only 15 of the 39 starters complete the course, with 18 of the athletes ending up in hospital.

Paavo Nurmi **(RIGHT)** was the dominant figure in athletics during the 1920s and into the 1930s, but by the time the Olympics was held in his home country, he was a reclusive figure. Finland's Prime Minister Urho Kekkonen persuaded Nurmi to take part in the opening ceremony, and the crowd rose in appreciation of the great man on July 19, 1952, at Helsinki's Olympic Stadium, as he lit the flame **(BELOW AND OPPOSITE RIGHT)**.

He had been unable to defend his 10,000 metres title as the Finnish selectors had decided to vary who was in which race, so when he returned to Finland he then set a new world record, a mark that would last 13 years and which meant he held the 1500 metres, mile, 3000, 5000 and 10,000 world records simultaneously.

After a massively successful tour of the US in 1925, Nurmi struggled with Achilles problems and found the shorter distances less to his liking. But his winning ways continued, including a story which many saw as a great sporting moment. At the 1928 Olympics in Amsterdam he again won the 10,000 metres, but an injury sustained in the steeplechase ruined further gold prospects.

In his heat for the 3000 metre steeplechase he fell at the water jump, spraining his hip and injuring his foot. France's Lucien Duquesne stopped to help him up, and Nurmi paced his opponent through the field and offered him the heat win… only for the Frenchman to refuse. In the 5000 and steeplechase finals a clearly injured Nurmi still managed to take silver.

In July 1931 Nurmi broke the world record for the rarely run two miles, becoming the first man to finish that in less than nine minutes, and planned a career swansong at the 1932 Los Angeles Olympics, but he was disqualified shortly before the games when the International Olympic Committee, under pressure from Sweden and Germany, ruled that his expenses claims were inflated.

It was the end on an era… but a final note should perhaps be made that the reclusive Nurmi was persuaded by his country's Prime Minister Urho Kekkonen to carry the Olympic torch into the stadium for the 1952 Helsinki games.

If peerless Paavo had shown the way, the next decade would show runners from all over the world that the four minute barrier was tantalisingly close, and it was perhaps only the coming of global conflict which delayed the breaking of it until that day in Oxford six decades ago.

As a boy, France's Jules Ladoumegue had pictures of Nurmi on his wall and he studied the Finn's training whenever he could. He was raised by an aunt and uncle following the death of his father just before he was born in 1906, and of his mother just 17 days after his birth.

As a 12-year-old he was apprenticed as a gardener to an architect who had land alongside a horse racing track, and it was his study of the horses' running techniques which influenced the young Jules' distinctive style.

John Bryant quotes Ladoumegue as saying he "loved the (horses') stride. I observed attentively their leg movements. I owe to them the high knee lift that was part of my style." ▶

A talented 5000 metre runner in his youth, he dropped down in distance and in 1928 began working with the coach Charles Poulenard. Ladoumegue was always a highly-strung character and would often vomit before or after a race… or sometimes both, and Poulenard would often have to drag his nervous runner to the start line. However, nothing could deny his talent, and with 1500 metres being predominant in France rather than the mile, it was in this event where dramatic time improvements were seen in 1928… just in time for the Amsterdam Olympics.

He lowered his 1500 metres time from 3:58 in June to 3:52.2 in the French Championship later that summer, this effort ranking him as the third fastest man ever over the distance. The final in the Netherlands saw more Finns provide the opposition, with Ladoumegue up against Eino Purje and Harri Larva, and it was the latter who prevailed, the Frenchman taking silver, and a lot of criticism back home that he lacked a 'kick' finish.

The following year he was beaten by AAAs champion Cyril Ellis, a very underrated athlete from Nottinghamshire, as well as Olympic champ Larva again, both in high profile events, and both by being out-sprinted. However, Ladoumegue was entering that 'purple patch' of form which top athletes hit, and was virtually unbeatable for a couple of seasons from 1930, beating Ellis in a mile event and world 1500 metres record holder Otto Pelzer over the metric distance.

He was in record-breaking form, and at the 450 metre track at Stade Jean Bouin in Paris he made an attempt on Peltzer's 3:51 world best. With Sera Martin, Jean Keller and Luigi Beccali setting the pace and pushing him on he crossed the line in 3:49.2, the first man to dip under

ABOVE: Jules Ladoumegue was a highly-strung but brilliant runner.

3:50 for the 1500 metres. Further world records were set at 1000 and 2000 metres over the next year, then on October 4, 1931, at his favourite Jean Bouin track, he made an attempt on Nurmi's mile record.

After two false starts, the field of seven Frenchmen propelled Ladoumegue to the verge of history… 'all' that was left was for a man who was 1.3 seconds down on Nurmi's time with 440 yards to go to claw it back. He did it, and more, taking 1.2 seconds off the Finn's record mark, and lowering the record to 4:09.2.

He said: "(On the last lap) I felt fresher than ever before. I lengthened my stride, stuck out my chest, raised my head. Going through 1500 I heard them shout 3:52.4. I knew then I was going to do better than Nurmi."

With the Los Angeles Olympics close at hand, Ladoumegue was then banned by the French Athletic Federation for receiving illegal payments. His career ended in the same way as Nurmi's had, with accusations of professionalism, and despite efforts by both men to hold a series of paid races in the US, their best days were over and the races never happened.

This isn't a history of the Olympic Games, we are not tracing the 1500 metre champions – although out of interest Italy's Beccali, part of that Ladoumegue 1500 record run, was the man who took the gold in LA.

Instead this is a story of the mile, and the next man to take centre stage was another of those great talents who perhaps never achieved his full potential on the track during this strict amateur era, and there are even claims that this New Zealander broke the four minute barrier during secret time trials.

Jack Lovelock was born in New Zealand in 1910, and similar to Nurmi and Ladoumegue he suffered family tragedy early, as his father died when Jack was just 13. Even by that age he was proving a talented sportsman, excelling at rugby and boxing, but running was where his heart lay and his worked tirelessly to develop a smooth and efficient style.

He excelled at school and was a Rhodes Scholar, travelling to Oxford to study medicine, and it was there that he impressed some knowledgable athletes and coaches, including Jerry Cornes and coach Bill Thomas, with his style and also the times he was recording. Of course the popular image of such Oxbridge athletes is that they were relaxed and carefree… and that training, especially hard, meticulous training, the type of work Nurmi would have put in, was not for them. Lovelock perhaps wanted to fit in with the crowd, so much of his hard graft was done in secret, running alone at night. ▶

LEFT: New Zealander Jack Lovelock was a medical student who studied at Oxford… a combination which obviously helped produce good milers. Some claim he broke four minutes during training.

BELOW: Lovelock (467) moves past American Glenn Cunningham (746) and Italy's Luigi Beccali in the 1936 Olympic final.

SWEET CHARIOTS

One of the most significant Olympic Games when it comes to middle distance running was that of 1924 in Paris, as it saw the first man to win both Olympic gold at the 1500 metres and also feature on our list of world mile record holders – the legend from Finland Paavo Nurmi.

'Peerless Paavo' took both 1500 and 500 metres, plus the cross country and team cross country, while fellow Finns Ville Ritola won the 10,000 metres and steeplechase and Albin Stenroos was victorious in the marathon.

But for many Britons, this is the 'Chariots of Fire Games', and often their first introduction to sporting legends such as Nurmi, as well as Harold Abrahams and Eric Liddell, the heroes of the 1981 Hugh Hudson movie.

Of course the Hollywood treatment means anyone taking their athletics history from the film should also take a pinch of salt when it comes to some of the key facts.

For example:
- Eric Liddell's late decision not to run in the 100 metres because the heat was on a Sunday was actually known about months in advance.
- The Great Court Run in which Abrahams beats Lord Lindsay never took place. However, Lord Burghley, upon whom Lindsay was based, did complete the challenge in 1927.
- Lindsay's butler placed glasses of champagne on hurdles to help improve his technique – in fact Burghley used matchboxes, and it was a very effective and scientific coaching approach.

But that was Hollywood, and the main point of the film was perhaps to showcase these real-life inspirational characters, and that's certainly what it did as far as Abrahams and Liddell were concerned.

And of course one of the central characters in the film was a man who features large in the history of the mile, 'Sam' Mussabini. His brilliance and innovation did not just help Abrahams, as featured elsewhere in this publication, Albert Hill was coached to glory by Mussabini.

ABOVE LEFT: Stade Olympique Yves-du-Manoir – or Stade Colombes to the locals – was the Olympic stadium in 1924 and host to the 'Chariots of Fire' games. It hosted rugby union and football internationals until the 1970s when the Parc des Princes was built.

ABOVE: Eric Liddell was one of the central characters in Chariots of Fire. In fact it was he who introduced Mussabini to Harold Abrahams.

BELOW: Harold Abrahams won gold in 1924 and was coached by the enigmatic Sam Mussabini.

ABOVE: Two record holders, one great race – Jack Lovelock beat Glenn Cunningham in the 1936 Olympics, and it was the American who would break the Kiwi's world mile best.

BELOW: Britain's Sydney Wooderson was perhaps an unlikely-looking hero, but this world record holder was an inspiration to young Roger Bannister.

What he brought to the middle distance events was a rigorous analysis that perhaps only a medical student could – two decades before medical man Roger Bannister would grace the same tracks. Lovelock kept diaries and recorded his physical condition as well as times, training regimes, diet etc.

In 1932, with the Olympics in Los Angeles on the horizon, Lovelock was keen to put himself in the frame for selection by New Zealand and in the race between Oxford University and the AAAs at Iffley Road he won in a time of 4:12, almost nine seconds better than his previous personal best. With the first and last 440 yards each being run under a minute, and the third 440 in 71 seconds, there was a massive variation in pace... so if he had held Nurmi's even pace philosophy what could have happened? What it did do was propel Lovelock to the Olympics, and with no little expectation.

In the end his LA experience was to end in disappointment, trailing well down the field in the final, but he was analysing everything, such as the effect the long voyage had on his fitness, the schedule of races and how to cope with it, and how to 'peak' for certain events.

The following year, on July 15, Lovelock was part of a combined Oxbridge team competing in the US and came up against Bill Bonthron from Princeton. There they both went under the former world record, Lovelock finished a second ahead of his American rival and lowering the world best by a massive margin – taking it down to 4:07.6.

A report in the *New York Herald Tribune* said: "(It makes the) four-minute mile seem just around the corner – or at least at that time when Lovelock finds the conditions as perfect in every detail as they were today, with a runner of equal stature to force the pace all the way as Bonthron did."

It's at this point that the stories again diverge, with a nod to Lovelock's next great achievement on the athletics track. The New Zealander won the gold medal in the 1500 metres at the Berlin Olympic Games, setting a world record of 3:47.8 in the final, and beating a class field in the process, with only Britain's Sydney Wooderson missing due to a fractured foot. Glenn Cunningham, Cornes and Beccali were all taken by surprise when with 300 metres to go, Lovelock – normally expected to leave his burst until quite late – made an early break for the line. His opponents were caught out and Lovelock was champion.

If Lovelock perfected the art of 'peaking' for races and events, he distracts from another great runner, a consistent runner, and the man who lowered the New Zealander's record within a year – Glenn Cunningham.

Born in 1909 in Kansas, the man nicknamed the Iron Horse of Kansas was badly burned as a child, and his legs were nearly amputated. But with an iron will he not only learned to walk again, but to run... and could he run. Lovelock often wrote about the strength of

Cunningham and when he competed at the 1936 Olympics he was voted Most Popular Athlete by his peers, just ahead of his room-mate Jesse Owens.

Before that, on June 16, 1934, at the first Princeton Invitational Games, Cunningham took on Bonthron and Gene Venzki in an epic mile. With more than 25,000 in the crown, and thousands of others having reportedly been turned away, Cunningham destroyed the opposition with a first lap just under 62 seconds, a second lap of 64, a third lap again under 62 and a final lap under a minute. It was close to Nurmi's ideal of even pace, and took the world best mark down to 4:06.8... ever closer to four minutes.

Cunningham's consistency was remarkable and the speculation over four minutes grew even stronger when in an indoor race he won in a remarkable time of 4:04.4... obviously with no wind and on a smooth wooden track. But as indoor times were not recognised by the sanctioning body, his outdoor time remained as the world best mark... until a very unlikely looking Briton took the record away.

Born in August 1914, Sydney Wooderson was a stark contrast to the well-muscled Cunningham, standing 5ft 6in, weighing in at nine stone and peering through his spectacles as he ran. But appearances were deceptive, and Londoner Wooderson became the first British schoolboy to run the mile in less than 4:30 when he was still 18.

Although the Olympic Games featured the 1500 metres, the British Empire Games, now known as the Commonwealth Games, in those days featured a one mile event, and it was there at White City in London where he announced himself to the world, finishing a close second to Jack Lovelock in 1934, and taking the notable scalp of Jerry Cornes in the process.

It's at this point that we are reintroduced to a former 'great' of British middle distance running, as Albert Hill, double Olympic champion from the 1920 games, was the coach who helped transform the raw talent of articled solicitor's clerk Wooderson into this deceptive dynamo with a blistering finish.

With a string of fine performances in 1935, the Olympic year promised to be a good one for Wooderson, and he started well by lowering his own British mile record, out-sprinting Lovelock in the process, and the New Zealander named the Briton as a man to be feared in the Olympics. However his hopes were dashed when he turned his ankle in a rabbit hole while out for a Sunday walk. The injury proved far worse than first feared and although he went to Berlin, Wooderson was eliminated in the 1500 metres heats.

The next year, injury healed, Wooderson entered the history books for ever, and yet his initial target that August day at Motspur Park was to attempt to lower the British mile record.

Conditions were perfect, and in the crowd that day was Walter George, the man who had run 4:12¾ in 1886. In a handicap race, Wooderson started on scratch with pacemaker Reg Thomas setting off 10 yards ahead and towing Wooderson through 880 yards in 2:02.6. His final time of 4:06.4 had beaten Cunningham's record, and the unlikely hero was carried shoulder high by the crowd.

Further medal chances eluded Wooderson as he missed the 1938 Empire Games due to exam commitments, and with war looming, the four minute barrier was safe from any further attempts by Britain's athletic star. He served as a radar operator during the Second World War and contracted rheumatic fever in 1944. Despite doctors' predictions that he would not run again, his reserves of strength prevailed and just after the war he actually ran his fastest mile, 4:04.2... but by then the record had moved on, and into neutral Sweden. ∎

> *"Sydney Wooderson was a stark contrast to the well-muscled Cunningham, standing 5ft 6in, weighing in at nine stone and peering through his spectacles as he ran."*

ABOVE: Deceptively powerful, Sydney Wooderson took the mile record down to 4:06.4 in 1937, ran a faster time after the war, but lost his 'peak' years to the global conflict.

Swede success

... then to the very edge

The Second World War claimed the lives of many great sportsmen, including rugby's Prince Obolensky **(BELOW LEFT)** and American Footballer Jack Lummus **(RIGHT)**.

We'll never know what would have happened to the world mile record if war hadn't overtaken Europe and the world in 1939. Many are convinced the four minute barrier would have been smashed a decade before it finally was.

Quite rightly sport took a back seat during those tumultuous years when millions of lives were lost, and when sporting competition did occur it was often as entertainment to raise the morale of a suffering public, whichever side of the conflict they were on.

In Britain the football leagues were cancelled, and instead regional competitions were held, with professional players serving in the military and often guesting for teams near where they were based. Of course many athletes on all sides of the conflict and from all sports were killed, injured or lost their 'peak' years, and sports such as rugby union saw numerous stars killed, including New Zealand international winger Donald Cobden, who died during the Battle of Britain, and the Russian-born England star Prince Alexander Obolensky who died in a training accident while serving as a pilot with the RAF.

Numerous American sporting stars died, such as baseball player Elmer Gedeon who was shot down over France, American footballer Jack Lummus – who was killed during the war in the Pacific – and athlete Foy Draper, a member of the relay squad alongside Jesse Owens during the 1936 Olympics.

The war was also a time of sporting unity, and in rugby league, which we have already seen was drawing crowds since its inception in the late 19th century, the normal leagues were abandoned, and instead Yorkshire and Lancashire competitions played. There was also a remarkable coming together of the rival codes, when a rugby union team played a rugby league side in two matches held to raise funds for the Red Cross. Both games were to union rules, league won both.

When the Second World War began Sydney Wooderson was holder of the world mile record, set on that great day at Motspur Park, and he competed sporadically during the war, travelling the length and breadth of Britain to draw crowds and raise both morale and money for the war effort. But the tracks were often poor, he was obviously unable to train to the same level as before the war, and with rationing in place there was never any question of serious times or record attempts being made, there simply wasn't an appetite for such things. No major championships were held in Britain and any meetings held were organised by the services or schools.

Wooderson served as a firefighter during the Blitz, then was called up for the Army, but with his poor eyesight it was difficult to find the right role for him. When he was struck down by rheumatic fever in 1944, many feared Wooderson would never run again, and especially not at the highest level.

However, one nation would take the 'English mile' to the very verge of the four minute barrier during those war years, and that was neutral Sweden… through the efforts of two men whose names were as linked together as Ovett and Coe would be four decades later – Gunder Haegg and Arne Andersson.

It's perhaps a bit too easy to say that the Swedes only flourished because the rest of the world was at war, life is never as black-and-white as ➤

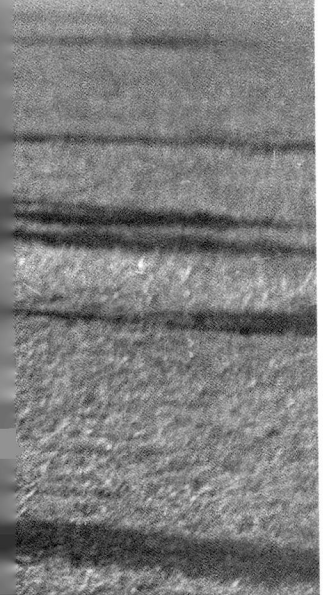

that, and even if there had been no conflict it's likely that Haegg and Andersson would have risen to the top. There were plenty of nations with top-class runners who continued athletic competition during the war years – after invasion by Germany, author Bob Phillips points out that France and Denmark re-established some semblance of athletics 'normality', while other nations such as Italy and Hungary were allies of Germany, and of course the US did not enter the war until after the attack on Pearl Harbor in 1941, and that nation had a fine record of producing top milers and men such as Blaine and Wayne Rideout, Chuck Fenske and Louis Zamperini.

So the emergence of the two Swedes would probably have happened anyway, especially as each showed massive talent as a child.

Haegg, born in Albacken in 1918, had already proved himself a promising youngster at local and regional level then received an extra inspiration through the efforts of a national hero, that man being 1936 Olympic 5000 metre bronze medallist Henry Jonsson-Kalarne.

Haegg's teenage victories were causing a stir, not least with his proud father Nils, and legend has it that when the pair were working as part of a lumberjack gang in the forests – the type of training which might have made Arnold Jackson shudder – Gunder's father measured out a 1500 metres track over the rough ground. John Bryant recalls the tale of how 17-year-old Gunder, being timed by his father using an alarm clock, ran the course in 4:45, a top class time for such conditions… and that it was only years later that Nils admitted he had deducted 30 seconds, as he hadn't wanted to discourage his talented son.

But Haegg's progress was interrupted when he became ill with double pneumonia, and he remained a 'promising talent' while others in Sweden rose more quickly to prominence, chief among them being Arne Andersson.

Just 14 months older than Haegg, Andersson had a very different background, but one massive similarity was the encouragement of his family. Born in Trollhattan, he trained to be a teacher and during that time made a name for himself as a young athlete, becoming the first Swede to break 3:50 for the 1500 metres in July 1939 in a match against old rivals Finland. His 3:48.8 was only a second shy of Jack Lovelock's world best, set at the Berlin Olympics.

Henry Jonsson-Kalarne, by no means an 'old man' at age 27, lowered the national 1500 record to 3:48.7, and his training partner Haegg – who had luckily recovered from his illness – equalled Andersson's time.

Kalarne and Haegg had been training at the remote centre of Valadalen, a skiing and sports centre located several hundred miles north of Stockholm and which utilised the natural forest environment. Athletics coach Gosta Olander was advocating what would be translated as 'speedplay', and taken on by Swedish Olympic coach Gosta Holmer it developed into a method which many later analysed and pored over.

A typical two hour session may have included a gentle warm-up, followed by steady hard speed for a couple of kilometres, then quick walking, easy running and hard sprints, uphill, downhill and using the natural forest tracks. While many nations worked solely on a track, the Swedes used their forests.

From 1941 the Swedish men went on a record-breaking spree that would last years. On August 10 that year, Haegg beat Lovelock's 1500 metre world record, finishing just ahead of Andersson in a time of 3:47.6, while the latter man headed the world mile rankings, and the following summer Haegg lowered the mile record to 4:06.2 – he had been banned for 10 months for

ABOVE: Arne Andersson (right) held the world mile record three times during a golden period for Swedish athletics.

LEFT: Gunder Haegg, was considered a hot favourite to take the mile world record below four minutes, but that scourge of 20th century athletics, 'professionalism', meant he and fellow countryman Andersson fell just shy… and it was Haegg's record which would fall in 1954.

expenses irregularities, and it was his first race of the season following a hard winter and spring of training.

At the Slottsskogsvallen track in Gothenburg on July 1, 1942, Olle Pettersson led them through the first lap in 58.8, the halfway point was reached in 2:02 and Haegg took over just after the bell was reached in 3:05.8. Andersson pushed Haegg every step of the way up the home straight and the watches stopped at 4:06.1, but the time was rounded up to 4:06.2 for official purposes.

Andersson attempted to break the record just 10 days later in Stockholm and he was ahead of schedule for most of the race, before finally crossing the line with a share of the world record.

The amazing sequence of record breaking continued, and over a variety of distances. On July 17 Haegg smashed 1.8 seconds off his 1500 metre record, and after already claiming the two mile record, he then took eight seconds off Kalarne's 3000 metre world best – finishing in a time of 8:01.2

On September 4, in a match against Germany, Haegg again reclaimed the mile record for himself, with another staggering performance. The leader went through the first lap in 56 seconds, a suicide pace, but Haegg wasn't too far off in 57.2, they went through the half mile in 2:00.2 and hit the bell at 3:04.2, before Haegg accelerated and crossed the finish line in a superb new world record of 4:04.6.

It's easy to concentrate too much on Haegg, though he remains one of all-time greats. The world record holder took a cargo ship to the US in 1943 in order to face the best runners on the far side of the Atlantic, and while he was away the world record was lowered by the widest margin since Nurmi had smashed Taber's record two decades earlier.

Andersson had been training hard and trying to improve his finishing speed by working with 400 metre runners, while losing none of his endurance. So he was in great shape for the event in Gothenburg which saw unheralded Arne Ahlsen set the perfect pace of 58 seconds for the first lap, 1:59.8 for the 880 yards and 3:02 for the three-quarter. ➤

THE UNBROKEN SPIRIT

Another athletics star, and his remarkable story, is set to get the Hollywood treatment... this time at the directorial hands of Angelina Jolie.

Louis Zamperini was one of a host of promising US athletes in the late 1930s, and when he ran 4:08.3 for the mile in 1938, his coach predicted great things, including that he'd be the first man to run under four minutes.

However, war intervened and Zamperini joined the air force. After his bomber crashed in the Pacific in 1943, Captain Zamperini spent 47 days alone in a life raft followed by more than two years as a Japanese prisoner of war.

During that time his weight dropped from 11st 11lb to 5st 9lb, and author John Bryant recounts how once his pedigree of having raced in the Olympics was discovered, Zamperini was forced to race against Japanese athletes.

"They wanted to show their runners could defeat me. I had no desire to compete, but was given to understand that if I did not run, not only I, but the whole camp, would suffer."

The story continues that pride kicked in, and the American overtook his opponents who, desperate to prove their superiority, extended the race. But he pulled further and further ahead until the 'race' was called off.

After the war Zamperini struggled with alcohol and post-traumatic stress disorder, but managed to turn his life around and went on to create the Victory Boys Camp, which is dedicated to helping troubled youngsters.

Now aged 97 and living in Olean, New York state, the movie Unbroken will tell his amazing life story.

Andersson scorched through the final lap in 59.1 to lower the record to 4:02.6, fully two seconds below the previous best, and just a tantalizing margin from the four minute barrier. Rune Gustafsson, who finished that race in second place, also beat the old record, so while Haegg was out of the country he was now the third best miler in Sweden!

Haegg continued his tour of the US throughout the summer, and put in some excellent performances in beating the best young talent in the States, while raising funds for the US war effort in the process, but he was more than aware of Andersson's record-breaking form, which included a 3:45 1500 metres. The following season was another classic, with Haegg, who by now worked in a clothes store after leaving the fire service, against teacher Andersson. Haegg broke his compatriot's 1500 metre record by two seconds in July, a second ahead of Andersson, and broke records and other runners' hearts all the way up to 5000 metres.

But Andersson was not outclassed, and on June 28, 1944, inflicted Haegg's first defeat in 56 races when beating him over 1500 metres Stockholm.

The mile was next, and in Malmo on July 18 the two faced off in front of a capacity crowd. There were three other runners, but the audience was there for one thing… and they were not to be disappointed. Lennart Strand led the race at a good pace, 56.8 for lap one, 1:56 for 880 yards, with Haegg close behind, and Andersson on his rival's shoulder. Haegg reached the three-quarter mark at 2:59.4 and pressed on, but Andersson was looming and eventually overtook him in the home straight, crossing the finish line in 4:01.6, with Haegg just 0.4 behind.

There was one final push from the Swedes, virtually a year after that epic 1944 encounter, and much happened in the intervening 12 months, including another trip to the US by Haegg. Both men ran a massive number of races – which would prove

BELOW: What could have been... Arne Anderson raced against Britain's Sydney Wooderson in the immediate aftermath of the Second World War. The British champion had been unable to race competitively for perhaps his best years, and the competition these two and Gunder Haegg should have enjoyed might well have brought that sub-four far sooner.

to be their undoing – but that last hurrah in terms of this story of the mile took place on July 18, again in Malmo. With a very quick opening lap and a halfway mark of 1:58.5, both men again looked in good form. Haegg again led at the bell, and again Andersson, king of the kick finish, loomed large. Andersson drew level in the home straight… but this time Haegg had the reserves to push on and win, in a time which was rounded up to 4:01.4.

It emerged later that a gun cartridge case had become embedded in Andersson's spikes, and with their shoes being so light, any such imperfection was always going to have a knock-on effect. Some claim it cost Andersson not just his record, but also the chance to dip under four minutes, as he was unable to finish with his usual blistering speed. That, again, is one of history's 'what if' moments.

The final time the two met on the track, in the September of 1945, the rumours of professionalism were too strong to be ignored. Strand actually won that final race which saw the great two go head-to-head, and the following year Sweden's governing body had banned both Haegg and Andersson for breaking rules over appearance money. They were 27 and 28, and perhaps approaching the peak years of their careers, with an Olympic games just a couple of years away.

The previous mile record holder, Sydney Wooderson had certainly had his peak years removed and it was only after the end of the war that he was able to compete against his Swedish rivals. What would have happened had Wooderson been able to run against Haegg and Andersson over the previous six years is purely speculation, as is what he could have done given facilities to train to his potential and a diet to match.

Haegg and Andersson pushed each other on to record after record, Andersson being a superb finisher, Haegg often remembered as the greater – it was a rivalry which Britons would replicate nearly four decades later when Ovett and Coe were in their pomp. But if Wooderson had been thrown into the mix as well, perhaps Bannister's place in history would have been taken by a different Briton, or one of the superb Swedes.

At the end of that summer of 1945, the Swedes competed at the White City Stadium in London, Haegg winning the two miles, and Andersson taking on and beating Wooderson. The Briton raced again against Andersson in Gothenburg, finishing second but in his best ever mile time of 4:04.1 as he pushed the Swede every stride of the way.

It's easy to see the next few years as being a 'black hole' in terms of middle distance running, of course it wasn't, but in terms of the tale of the mile it was a period in which the four minute myth was perhaps at its height, because the record was so close… and yet so far.

Lennart Strand was the best of the Swedes having avoided the expenses scandal, compatriot Henry Eriksson was not far behind, while Americans such as Gil Dodds and Roland Sink were competitive, plus Dutch runner Willy Slijkhuis and Britain's best young hope going into the 1948 ➤

> *"It emerged that a gun cartridge case became embedded in Andersson's spikes. Some claim it cost not just the record, but also the chance to dip under four minutes."*

ABOVE: John Landy came close time and time again to breaking the four minute barrier ahead of Bannister.

BELOW: American Wes Santee was a 'nearly man' of the mile, coming so close to taking the record, but in the end never breaking the barrier. Here he wins an event in the rain at London's White City.

Olympics, Bill Nankeville. But none were coming near Haegg and Andersson's marks.

Eriksson won gold in the 1948 1500 metres final, but there were no real threats to the mile world best, and in the US, the college runners were more concerned with winning than setting records.

By the end of 1950, seven of the top 10 milers were Swedish, there were two Americans – Bill Hulse and Gil Dodds, and the sole Briton, Sydney Wooderson, but now there was a new target, the 1952 Olympics in Helsinki, and a new group of young athletes coming to the fore, including Roger Bannister, a man who had shown promise before London and who some thought would have benefitted from the experience of the games.

However, Bannister's tale is to come… indeed the battle between Bannister and some significant other protagonists will dominate these pages to come, and the first of these is a man who had as his inspiration the last American to hold the world mile record.

David Wesley (Wes) Santee was born in Kansas in 1932, the same part of the world as 'Iron Horse' Glenn Cunningham, and grew up on a farm. If the Swedes Haegg and Andersson were from supportive families, the same could hardly be said for Santee and it's said that he rebelled by running when his ranch hand father wanted him to work. Whatever the story, athletics seemed to be the young Santee's ticket out, and he set state records as a youngster in the mile, two miles and cross country.

With the American college system so dominant, Santee's University coach Bill Easton was always looking for victories and regular racing, but it seemed to build the young Santee's fitness and competitive edge, if not helping his ability to break records. He was selected for the 1952 Olympics… but unfortunately, as often seems to be the way with athletics governing bodies and officialdom, he had been selected for the 5000 metres and not his favoured 1500.

After finishing second in the 5000 at the US Olympic trials, he was pulled off the track at the start of the 1500 trial and told by officials that he wasn't allowed to race… he never received a full explanation as to why. At the Helsinki games he failed to reach the 5000 final, while Luxembourg's Josy Barthel won the 1500 in a photo-finish with American Bob McMillen, whom Santee had often beaten in college races. Bannister was fourth behind the German Werner Lueg.

Santee will go down as one of the 'nearly men' of mile running. It was he, and John Landy, who spurred Bannister's efforts even further in 1954, and Santee's 4:02.4 set the cat among Bannister's proverbial pigeons when his final two laps were recorded as 58.2 and 58.9 during a track meet in California, but he was never to crack that elusive barrier, his fastest miles being 4:00.5 (set in 1955), 4:00.6, 4:00.7, 4:01.2 and 4:01.3. Just a month after Bannister's mile record he broke Lueg's world 1500 metres best.

The 6ft 1in tall Santee would often have to run three races in a day for his college, and not long after that personal best mile time he was suspended for a year by his governing body, the Amateur Athletic Union (AAU), in a dispute over his amateur status – the AAU claiming he had 'broken training' in Europe the previous summer.

That winter he broke the world indoor record for the mile twice, the second time setting the 1500 mark along the way to a 4:03.8 finish. In 1956, with Melbourne's Olympics close at hand, he was again accused by the AAU of accepting excessive expenses from promoters. This time his running career was over.

Of the other candidates who could break the four minute barrier, and there were indeed many 'possibles' ➤

John Landy was a superb front runner, and the Australian's tactic was often to run the finish out of his opponents.

and some 'probables'. The man upon whom many had their money would later become the 26th Governor of the Australian state of Victoria – indeed there's something about milers and politics which does seem to mix, especially in the latter half of the 20th century.

John Michael Landy was born in 1930 into a prosperous, middle class Australian family. Not for him the economic travails which had forged the young Wes Santee, instead he attended one of the best schools in Australia, Geelong Grammar, and excelled academically as well as at a number of sports, including in the rough, tough Australian rules football. But it was while at college that he concentrated on the track as until that point he had mainly run in order to keep fit for football.

When he made the state athletics team in 1951, he decided to take the sport more seriously, and after winning the Combined Schools Mile in a time of 4:43, he was introduced to Percy Cerutty, the colourful and enigmatic coach who was already building quite a reputation. Fellow runner Don MacMillan was already part of Cerutty's squad of athletes, and he encouraged Landy to work with the coach too.

The elegant Landy made massive progress under the new regime. Within three weeks he ran 4:31 and after four months he had recorded a time of 4:17.

On November 10, 1951, Landy ran 4:14.6, which was faster than MacMillan's time to win that year's national championship, and by early 1952 the 21-year-old was attracting national attention, having run a 4:11 on January 12 at Melbourne. "Without his guidance and inspiration I couldn't even have approached the times I ran," Landy is quoted as saying.

MacMillan won the national championships that year though, and Landy was selected for the Helsinki Olympics… if he paid his own fare to Finland. The Landy family and the local community put their hands in their pockets and he was on his way to northern Europe, stopping off in Britain for some warm-up races.

Landy and MacMillan took on Britain's Bill Nankeville in a mile event, and it was the home athlete who won in 4:09.8, with Landy an impressive second in 4:11. He went on to improve his best with a 4:10, but in the Olympics he was disappointing and disappointed, finishing fifth in his heat.

After the games both Landy and Bannister were on the same team – as part of an exciting 4 x one mile relay race between the British Empire and the United States at London's White City, Wes Santee being on the US team.

Bannister ran a 4:09.8 and Landy 4:09.9 in the race and it was the end of a hard European season… but for one of the men, things were about to get better, a lot better.

Landy had learned many lessons from Helsinki, and prime among them were the training methods of the great Czech athlete Emil Zatopek who won the 5000, 10,000 and marathon at Helsinki and who had himself modelled his training techniques on what he could read about Paavo Nurmi. Landy also realised how much better the European running shoes were, and armed with such spikes and his new methods of interval training, he returned Down Under, and was running 4:08 miles in training sessions.

In December 1952, came a performance which rocked the world of athletics. At a club meeting in Melbourne Landy ran 4:02.1. It was the fastest time for seven years, the fastest since the Swedes during the war, and it placed him third on the all-time list with the fourth fastest time ever behind Haegg's 4:01.4 and 4:02,

and Andersson's 4:01.6. Landy had run the final three laps on his own, and despite the change in his training techniques introduced by the athlete himself, he still credited Cerutty, and was reported to have said: "Most of the credit must go to Perce."

However, Cerutty is understood to have gone ballistic, saying that if Landy had been capable of such a time then he had let his side down at the Olympics. Landy broke with Cerutty.

The race for the first sub-four was on, and Landy was leading the charge. In the first few weeks of 1953 he was again in stunning form.

"Landy was selected for the Helsinki Olympics… if he paid his own fare. His family and local community put their hands in their pockets."

Despite suffering from a cold, on January 3 he ran 4:02.4 on a far-from perfect Melbourne track and in gusty conditions, and his time at 1500 metres would have won the Olympic final the year before. Just three weeks later, on a grass track in Perth, he ran 4:04.2, but in an atmosphere of expectation, it was being seen by some as a failure.

Landy was facing his university final exams, and once done he threw himself into training for the new Australian season. In December he recorded a flat 4:02, and into 1954 his form saw a string of times which threatened the record… but never quite made it, with a 4:02.4 in January and another 4:02 in April.

By the end of the Australian season he had run under 4:06 nine times, and was preparing for a trip to Europe. In all those races Down Under he had done it with very little competition, surely being pushed by quality opposition in the northern hemisphere would see him dip below four minutes and break that record before anyone else… ∎

OPPOSITE PAGE: John Landy and Wes Santee were the main rivals to Bannister for ducking under four minutes, but neither could manage it through 1953 and the Australian summer of 1953/4.

ABOVE: Britain's Gordon Pirie won the first Emsley Carr Mile race against the much-fancied Wes Santee at London's White City, an event started in the hope of breaking the four minute barrier.

Roger Bannister set a new championship best for the mile in the AAAs event in 1951 at White City.

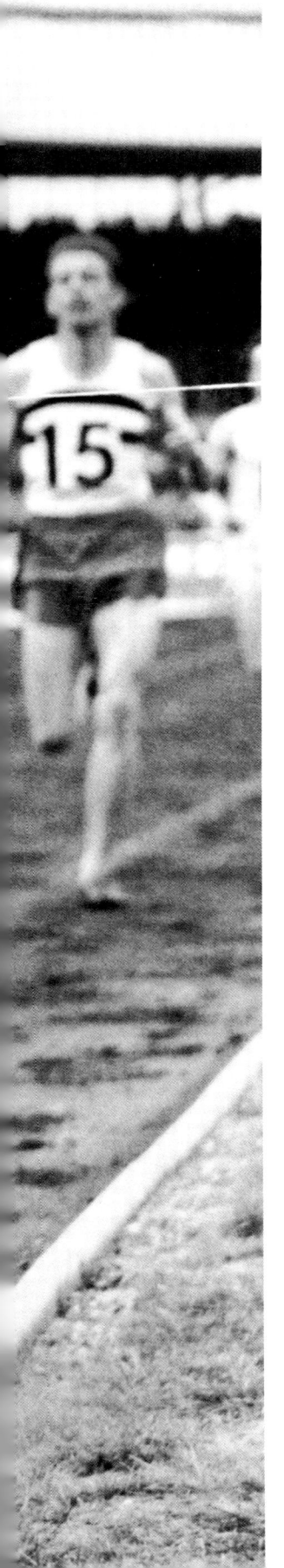

Doctor under orders...
and the three musketeers

It was a 'failure' which drove Roger Bannister to his greatest success – a success which lasted for just 46 days... and yet which would also last for ever. Yet his initial sporting inspiration was a wiry athlete who was robbed of his greatest years by the Second World War.

As described earlier, Sydney Wooderson was the pride of Britain on the track, and when he displayed true grit in taking on Arne Andersson at White City Stadium on August 6, 1945, the 54,000 sell-out crowd included Ralph Bannister and his 16-year-old son, Roger.

The young Bannister had been born in Harrow and the family moved to Bath when he was still a young child. Interviewed a decade ago, Bannister described how he was "always a great bundle of energy. Instead of walking, I would run. And so running, which is a pain to a lot of people, was always a pleasure to me because it was so easy".

He enjoyed success in his early races at school, especially in cross country events, and when he went up to Exeter College at Oxford University when aged just 17 – and with those memories of Wooderson fresh in his mind – he immediately signed up to join the athletics club.

He was a raw talent, and his first appearance in Oxford colours was that November in a cross country race in Kent when two generations would meet, as it was the only time Wooderson and Bannister competed against each other, the former mile record holder finishing third in the seven mile race, while the Oxford student finished fifth.

That winter was one of the harshest on record, and the old Iffley Road track, which in those days was competed on in a clockwise direction and was three laps to the mile, was snowbound for much of the winter. Bannister helped clear the ground so that training could continue, and when it came time for the match against Cambridge the following March he was picked for the mile race at the neutral White City Stadium in London, the same track he and his father had watched Wooderson race on just two years earlier.

The Cambridge team set out hard and Bannister simply hung on, running faster than he'd gone before over the distance, and at the bell he was tired... but still in touch.

It was then that many first saw what would become a familiar sight – the young Bannister kicked, then kicked again, with his long stride eating up the ground so that he eventually won by 20 yards against much more experienced runners.

He would say: "I felt a crazy desire to overtake the whole field."

His winning time was 4:30.8, and the press – with one eye on the following year's Games which had been awarded to London – started talking about him as an Olympic 'possible'.

And there was another familiar sight too... the shattered Bannister, slumped with exhaustion following his exertions.

With those London postwar Olympics approaching Bannister was selected as a 'possible' for the British ➤

April 1954, a month before the record, and Roger Bannister is deep in conversation with Gordon Pirie.

Olympic team, but the 19-year-old decided it was simply too soon. "I thought I wasn't ready," he said. "It was thought if you indulged in too much racing when you were too young, you could burn yourself out... I decided I would wait for the 1952 Olympics."

In the meantime, he was elected president of the Oxford University Athletic Club, and as part of his address to members he said he wanted to improve the club in a number of ways... with better coaching, with a revival of Oxbridge tours of America, and with a major overhaul of the Iffley Road track – getting rid of the massive dip on the back straight, changing the direction of running from clockwise to anti-clockwise (like the rest of the world), and a redesign so it became four laps to the mile rather than three.

Bannister was involved in the London Olympics... as an assistant to the administrator for the British team, and his claim to fame at those games was that when the national flags were distributed as teams marched into Wembley Stadium, the Union Flag wasn't there, so Bannister was given the job of finding one. He was forced to break a car window in order to get a flag and just make it back in time for the British team's entrance.

In 1949 Bannister won his third Oxford versus Cambridge clash, recording a time of 4:16.2, and in the US he recorded times of 4:11.9 and then 4:11.1 against the top American universities, each time running the final 440 yards in less than a minute

ABOVE: Bannister won the Benjamin Franklin Trophy in 1951 after winning in Philadelphia in 4:08.3.

LEFT: Flag Day – Roger Bannister back on the Iffley Road track in 1994. In the background the church flew the same flag as on the day he ran the first sub-four mile.

RIGHT: Bannister made his name as a student athlete at Oxford. In 1950 he won the mile in the annual Varsity encounter with Cambridge.

Bannister, a full-time medical student, had his own methods of training, and they were certainly light by today's standards, sessions lasting for only about 30 minutes three or four times a week. But for his scientific mind it was the optimum way to work, he targeted events and built for those, being careful not to burn out. He studied the methods of other athletes, and adapted them to fit in with his own schedule, so the programme and methods of Gunder Haegg were studied, just as much as those of fellow Oxford man Jack Lovelock, the hero of 1936, yet whose coach, Bill Thomas, Bannister found it virtually impossible to work with and learn from at Oxford just a decade-and-a-half later.

The following year, 1950, saw further improvements as he finished a relatively slow 4:13 mile on July 1 with a 57.5 last lap, then he ran the AAA 880 yards in 1:52.1, losing to Arthur Wint, and then a 1:50.7 for the 800 metres in taking a bronze medal at the European Championships at the Heysel Stadium in Brussels on August 26, his time equalling that of silver medal winner Marcel Hansenne and just two tenths behind British winner John Parlett, who ran a personal best to get the gold.

This relative lack of success spurred Bannister on and he trained more seriously, yet even so his training methods (and lack of a specific coach) were criticised as part of the reason for his biggest disappointment – the 1952 Olympic 1500 metres.

Going into that Olympic year he was moving up the world rankings and impressing those in the know. In the US in 1951 he won the Benjamin Franklin Mile in 4:08.3, while also that year a partnership began which would eventually deliver that record. Chris Chataway won that year's Oxford-Cambridge mile, and in the April during a three-quarter mile race Chataway set the pace before Bannister roared on to finish in 2:56.8, beating Sydney Wooderson's English record by almost three seconds.

In July of 1951 he took the scalp of defending champion and Britain's premier miler Bill Nankeville, winning in 4:07.8 at the AAA Championships at White City in front of a near-50,000 crowd.

But he wasn't unbeatable, with Yugoslavia's Andrija Otenhajmer taking the honours in a 1500 metres race in Belgrade that August. The home favourite won in 3:47.0 and ran the finishing burst out of Bannister by setting a gruelling pace, although the Briton did record a personal best to finish second in 3:48.4.

Experts couldn't agree who was favourite for Olympic gold in Helsinki, although the (partisan) McWhirter twins Norris and Ross, who published Athletics World, favoured Bannister, while others suggested the Germans Werner Lueg, Gunter Dohrow, Dutchman Willem 'Wim' Slijkhuis, or even Nankeville.

Bannister was happy with his preparations, running a 880 yard race in late May in 1:53.0, then a 4:10.6 mile time-trial on June 7, and at the AAA championships he entered the half-mile and won in 1:51.5.

However, any confidence was shattered when it was announced there would be an extra round for the 1500 metres, and the Briton knew this favoured runners who had far more 'in their legs' and deeper training sessions than he did. When he ran his semi-final, Bannister finished fifth to qualify, but said he felt "blown and unhappy". ➤

A fresh-faced Roger Bannister in March 1948.

BELOW: Bannister was well known for giving everything in his final 'burst' to the line, these famous images being those taken immediately after his sub-four mile.

The final on July 26 was a bit of a shock, being won in the final few yards by Josy Barthel of Luxembourg, with the first eight men all under the old Olympic record. Bannister was fourth, just outside the medals, but had set a British record in the process.

He later said: "(The extra round) was such a shock to me. I really didn't manage to give it my best, although I was in the fourth position in the last lap of the final, which was the position from which I would usually expect to unleash a finishing burst. I'm afraid there was nothing there.

"I had set my mind on winning the 1500 metres… my ambition was always to do what Lovelock had done. The reasons why I came fourth are unimportant. It was a reorganisation of the pattern of the races and my very slender training which let me down. I did not have the capacity to recover quickly."

"Instead of retiring I decided to go on for another two years while I was still a student… and the target of the four minute mile then came into view."

Of course, had Bannister won the Olympic gold in Helsinki, he would probably would have stepped away from the sport and the first sub-four mile would have been another athlete's… thus are the twists and turns of sport.

"Instead of retiring in order to devote myself to medicine, I decided to go on for another two years while I was still a student, working clinically in London.

"I decided I could just manage to fit running in with my medical studies until 1954," he said.

"The targets that would have justified this failure, as I saw it, were the Commonwealth Games – or Empire Games as they were then – and the target of the four minute mile then came into view."

With these targets now set, Bannister intensified his training and did harder intervals, and the form of John Landy certainly focused the mind. As described in Chapter 6, the Australian suddenly knocked several seconds off what everyone else was doing and made any record attempts urgent.

In Coronation year, 1953, Bannister started making real progress. On May 2 he made an attempt to break Sydney Wooderson's British mile record at Oxford, and paced by Chris Chataway, he ran 4:03.6, shattering Wooderson's 1945 best.

Then on June 27 came a controversial 'race', or even just a blatant record attempt. A mile race was inserted into the programme of the Surrey schools athletic meeting at Motspur Park. Australian Don Macmillan, ninth in the 1500 metres at Helsinki, ran 59.6 for the first lap and went through 880 yards in 1:59.7. He gave up into the third lap… and the 'problem' had been how to keep pushing Bannister along, after all, this was close to world record pace.

The solution the three found was ingenious, and controversial. Chris Brasher had jogged the race so far, allowing himself to be lapped so he could be a fresh pacemaker for the vital third Bannister lap. At the three-quarter mile Bannister was at 3:01.8, the record was in reach… but they fell short and he crossed the line in 4:02.0, a time bettered by only Andersson and Haegg. But there was fury, at the blatant 'pacemaking', at the secrecy of the event, and British officials would not allow this performance to stand as a national record. Years later Bannister said: "My feeling as I look back is one of great relief that I did not run a four-minute mile under such artificial circumstances."

The board's feelings were made clear in its statement which said the Motspur Park 'race' "had not been done in a bona fide competition according to the rules" and it did "not regard individual record attempts as in the best interests of athletics as a whole".

But 4:02 was still the time he had run, it was known he was close, and three men, Landy, Santee and Bannister were within tenths of a second of each other, and surely physically capable of breaking four minutes.

As described in our previous chapter, in early 1954, Landy made some more serious attempts at the distance, recording 4:02.4 in Melbourne, then twice stopping the watch at 4:02.6. With Landy's season Down Under ending in early April, and with the Australian heading the Scandinavia, time was of the essence, Bannister knew he had to make his attempt soon, and he had just the men to help him.

The next of the 'three musketeers' was Chris Brasher, a man of remarkable energy and drive, and who died aged 74 in 2003.

Oftem mentioned by the uninitiated as 'one of the men who helped Roger Bannister', instead he had a fantastic athletics career of his own… and then an equally remarkable post-running life, becoming an Olympic gold medallist and co-founder of the London Marathon, as well as an award-winning journalist, broadcaster and businessman.

Described as some as "stubborn" and "abrasive", he was also extremely modest of his talents, and decades after the record run he claimed he felt "something of a fraud", and that he was "a very ordinary athlete with very little to my personal credit", having found fame ➤

ABOVE: Chris Brasher never had the raw pace for the mile, and concentrated on the steeplechase. Here he follows his friend and fellow Briton John Disley over the water jump.

LEFT: Chris Brasher of Cambridge poses for the camera before the 1950 Varsity match at White City.

through Bannister's talent, but that self-opinion doesn't do justice to the man who was born in August 1928 in British Guyana, where his father had been posted. The young Chris attended Rugby school and St John's, Cambridge, where he won an athletics Blue.

Never the most gifted athlete, Brasher competed in the 3000 metres steeplechase at the 1952 Olympics, finishing next-to-last but taking on board many lessons from the way other athletes trained and prepared.

Working closely with coach Franz Stampfl, he went on to achieve success in his own right on the track following his 1954 claim to fame at Iffley Road, his greatest achievement actually starting with a 'favour' from a friend… as he managed to squeak into the British team for the Melbourne 1956 Olympics when John Disley, who had already been selected, paced him to the qualifying time.

In that event Down Under he was first across the finish line… but then almost immediately disqualified following a mid-race collision with the Norwegian Ernst Larsen. Brasher immediately appealed, and after some hesitation – perhaps because it may not have been a 'British' thing to do – the team manager supported him. Larsen himself confirmed nobody had obstructed him, and Brasher was declared Olympic champion.

After a very long evening celebrating with his friend Chris Chataway, Brasher had to rush to be in time to receive his medal. He later reflected he was perhaps the only Olympic champion to be "totally and absolutely slaughtered" when he received his medal.

A year later he become sports editor of the Observer, and was twice named Sportswriter of the Year, while in the early 1960s he worked for the BBC as a programme editor and producer, including on the Tonight programme.

But there was so much more to Brasher. While continuing his sports writing, he also co-founded the British Orienteering Federation, and in partnership with his fellow former athlete Disley formed a company called The Sweatshop, which sold athletics equipment. That business was eventually bought by Reebok in 1990.

But for hundreds of thousands of UK athletes, an event they take part in on the streets of London is down to Brasher's vision.

In the 1970s he took part in the New York City marathon and wrote in the Observer afterwards to ask if London had "the heart and hospitality to welcome the world?"

Persuading Observer editor Donald Trelford that the project could and should work, he then used his skills and persuasiveness to convince the local authorities and police to back him too, as well as ➤

ABOVE: Brasher enjoyed cross-country and competed in the Varsity clash on Wimbledon Common in 1947.

BELOW: Brasher leads the way in the steeplechase at the national championships of 1952.

RIGHT: 'Roar' emotion as Chris Brasher crosses the line to win Olympic gold in 1956.

56 FOUR MINUTE MILE

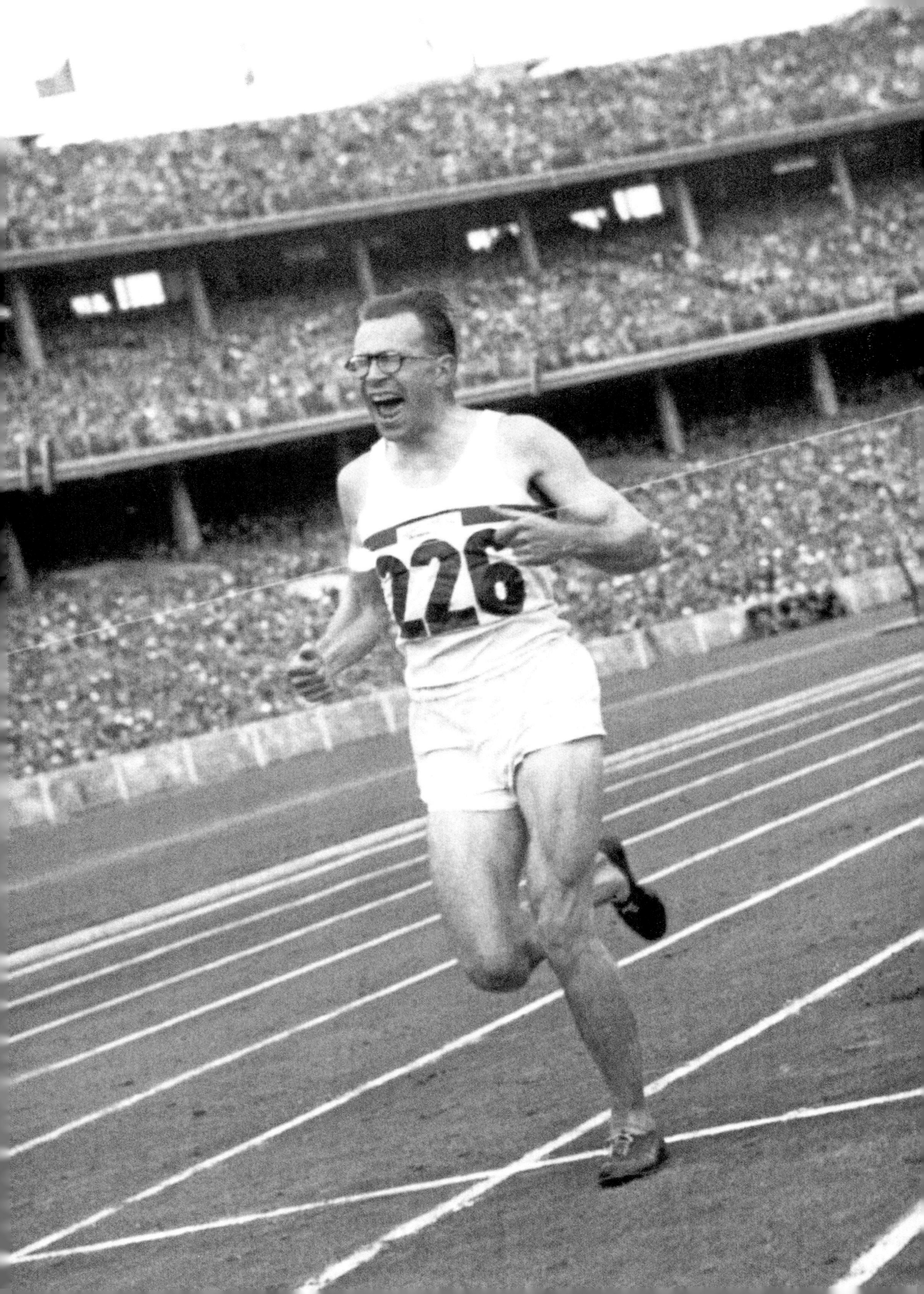
226

headline sponsor Gillette. On March 29, 1981 that dream became a reality when 8000 runners set off (including 52-year-old Brasher).

Brasher accepted a CBE when John Major was Prime Minister, having earlier refused one from Margaret Thatcher on the grounds that he "couldn't take it from that bloody woman. She did nothing for British sport".

The third on the Iffley Road triumvirate was another remarkable character, as alluded to in the introduction to this publication, and a man who should have been sharing the spotlight with his friend Roger Bannister this year before his death in January.

Christopher John Chataway was world 5000 metres record holder, television anchor man and reporter, Conservative MP, government minister, successful businessman and chairman of the Civil Aviation Authority… indeed as he once said himself, he "never made up my mind what (he) wanted to do".

After his death in 2014, Prime Minister David Cameron said: "Chris was one of a kind; throwing himself into every project and achieving so much in so many fields. We have lost a great Briton."

Born in January 1931, Chataway attended Sherborne School in Dorset and, after National Service, went up to Magdalen College, Oxford… where he followed in Roger Bannister's footsteps and became president of the University Athletic Club.

Chris Chataway, Derek Ibbotson and Gordon Pirie trailed in the wake of Vladimir Kuts in the 1956 Olympics 5000m final.

Another Chataway legacy, indirectly, is the Guinness Book of records… as when on leaving university he got a job with Guinness and Sir Hugh Beaver came up with the idea for the Guinness Book of Records. Chataway who suggested his old university friends Norris and Ross McWhirter as editors, knowing of their interest in statistics and facts.

Like many of his generation, his career at the very top of athletics was not top last too long, but it was glorious.

Another who competed at the Helsinki Olympics, his memories of that competition were also dominated by disappointment as in the final of the 5000 metres, after being passed by the great Emil Zatopek and two or three other athletes, he clipped the kerb and fell. Chataway managed to continue and finished in fifth place.

Bannister later said: "Chris had a very low boredom threshold and thought more or less of giving up after the disappointment of Helsinki. But he found with Franz (Stampf) and Chris Brasher he could keep his interest going."

But like Bannister, 1954 was a standout year… indeed, it was he who became the BBC's Sports Personality of the Year that year, the first time it had been presented, and he often put that down to one event – the race in which he set a new 5000 metres world record of 13 minutes 51.6 seconds in a televised race at White City. ➤

FAR LEFT & LEFT: Chris Brasher received the Sportsman of the Year Trophy for his efforts in 1956, and was made a CBE by the Queen in 1996.

BELOW: Chris Chataway was among the leading runners (along with Walter Hesketh and Roger Bannister) who represented Britain in Morocco in 1953.

BOTTOM: As chairman of Athletics UK's steering group Sir Chris Chataway (left) was key to discussions when the BBC announced in 1998 that it had won the rights to screen British athletics.

Chataway and Bannister were named as the sporting personalities of 1954 for their on-track feats.

> "Our friendship dated back more than half a century. We laughed, ran and commiserated together."
>
> *Roger Bannister*

Chataway beat Russia's Vladimir Kuts by a tenth of a second, having lost to the Soviet athlete at the European Championships final two weeks earlier. The fact the race was shown live on TV, attracting millions of viewers in the days long before multiple TV channels, did massive amounts to boost his popularity, in stark contrast to his effort on behalf of Bannister that May which was only seen by 1500 in the crowd and then relayed on film later.

By September 1955, Chataway became the first newsreader on Independent Television, and he then went on to compete in the Melbourne Olympics, finishing 11th in the 5000 metres. He joined the BBC's TV team as a commentator on current affairs, before eventually working on Panorama for four years.

He then made the switch into politics, and was a Conservative MP for North Lewisham between 1959 and 1964, rising to become a Parliamentary Private Secretary and junior Education Minister. He was elected again in 1969 after winning a by-election at

Chichester, and became the opposition spokesman on the environment, then in Ted Heath's government moved to the Department of Trade and Industry.
In 1974 he retained his Chichester seat in at the general election of February, but then did not seek re-election in the October election that year and retired from politics to concentrate on his business career, becoming managing director of Orion Bank, then in 1988 chairman of the Civil Aviation Authority.

After Chataway's death following a long battle with cancer in 2014, Roger Bannister said "he was one of my best friends. He was gallant to the end.

"Our friendship dated back over more than half a century. We laughed, ran and commiserated together. People will always remember him for the great runner he was but it shouldn't be forgotten that he had an extremely distinguished career off the track.

"My family and I will miss him sorely and our thoughts go out to his family and many friends who were so fond of him."

Sebastian Coe described Chataway as a 'Renaissance Man' and said: "He was a four-time world record holder, inspired Roger to the first sub four-minute mile, made two Olympic finals and won the Commonwealth Games title at three miles in Vancouver. He did all this on four training sessions, so had bags of natural talent.

"If he and Roger had not broken the four-minute mile, and it had gone to someone like Australia's John Landy, that distance would have had a different geographical feel."

It took three massive personalities, three massive friends, to work together and secure the record. Each has had a remarkable life and made a massive impact not just on athletics, but on the nation in many different ways. And the record itself… it was a barrier each knew would be beaten – as described in chapter 2.

But they were the first, and their names would forever be linked in history. ■

TOP LEFT AND ABOVE: One of his darkest days – Chris Chataway fell while challenging in the final of the 5000 metres at the Helsinki Olympics of 1952. As he tumbled the great Czech Emil Zatopek sprinted to take gold, beating France's Alain Mimoun into silver while German Herbert Schade finished third.

FOUR MINUTE MILE 61

This training don't stop...

Roger Bannister's success as the man to finally break through the four-minute barrier was a massive event in sporting history, but it can hardly be said to have been the culmination of generations of running knowledge distilled in a logical progression into one glorious moment.

For just as the old adage goes, you can put six economists in a room and come out with seven theories. Similarly the methods of training, practising and coaching were wide and varied... and always had been.

Bannister is, and certainly at the time in the 1950s was, portrayed as a man who 'went his own way', and as a medical student and then young doctor he brought his own scientific rigour and approach to how he felt he could get the best from himself.

As Bannister himself has said: "We didn't really know how to train in modern terms. There was this thing called 'burning yourself out'. I didn't want to burn myself out at 18, and I had a notion that if I looked after myself, trained carefully, I would go on improving, not by training two to three hours a day, but by training three quarters of an hour a day. It seemed to me logical that you could go on improving, and you didn't have to spend all day running."

Unlike his friends Chataway and Brasher, Bannister didn't really employ the services of a coach, although their mentor Franz Stampfl was perhaps the closest he had to one, and Bannister credits Stampfl as giving him the inspiration for taking on the record attempt on the day he did, beating Landy to the mark in the process.

Austrian-born Stampfl told Bannister: "If you have the opportunity – not a perfect opportunity – and you don't take it, you may never have another chance." As Bannister said years later: "It was that thought, I think, which eventually led me to attempt it."

The great athletes who had set records before Bannister had what could politely be called a 'varied' approach to the art of running. As described in chapter four, Captain Allardice, the great pedestrian of the early 19th century, had a rigorous training regime which apparently even included being woken at 4am so that he could 'enjoy' his final few hours' sleep in a hammock, the theory being that such an environment loosened his back and leg muscles and got him ready for his morning training run.

Years later and Lon Myers, seen by the Americans as an athletic wonder for his range of races – he ran the 100 yards in 10 seconds, the 440 in 48.6 and the mile in 4:22.6 – could be described as 'slapdash' in his training methods, relying instead on his racing programme to stay in shape. His pre-race days would often include staying up all night drinking and gambling.

The great Walter George, who went from amateur to professional, adapted his training to fit in with his work duties in a pharmacy. His unorthodox technique was to do what he called '100-up', which involved running in place with high knee lifts and springing, and he also took baths in brine. By 1882 George was running every morning and afternoon, gaining endurance from cross-country runs, slow runs of a mile or two, and faster sprints of 440 yards and short sprints.

On the track he used paced running as part of his training. He always ran a fast first lap as he was convinced that was the way to running a 4:12 mile – first lap 59, after lap two his schedule was 2:02, after lap three 3:08... and the final goal being 4:12... and it's said he kept the piece of paper for this 'perfect race' in his pocket all his life.

By the start of the 20th century, Britain's Joe Binks was a 'typical' cavalier amateur and his training took place one evening a week. ➤

LEFT: The training wisdom of Alfred Shrubb was a huge influence on the young Roger Bannister, who was given a book written by the great Victorian athlete.

LEFT: Austrian-born Franz Stampfl coached many of Britain's star athletes. In 1955 he and his Australian wife Patsy left the UK so he could coach at the University of Melbourne and organise a coaching scheme for the State of Victoria.

BELOW: Stampfl (in trademark flat cap), with Oxford's University athletes at White City.

John Bryant quotes Binks, who went on to work for the *News of the World*, as saying his training "was always light, I would run half-a-dozen 6 x 60-100 yard bursts of speed, and finish with a fast 220 or 300 yards."

Despite this, natural talent saw Binks set a British record of 4:16 4/5.

A fellow great runner of the era was Alfred Shrubb, a record holder with a range of distance from two miles up to 10. He was another who, in 1904, fell foul of amateur rules and was banned for being a professional. He later wrote a book on how to train and race... a publication which the young Roger Bannister was given by his father.

Shrubb never excelled in the mile, but certainly for his time was a revolutionary and sophisticated trainer, training hard and often running in time trials and at race pace.

And hard work was something the Americans were fond of when it came to their athletes. Of the many coaches in those turn-of-the-century days who could claim to have influenced the sport, few had the longevity of John 'Jack' Moakley, who became Cornell University's first full-time track coach in 1899... and held the post for 50 years.

Born in 1863, he worked well into his eighties and died just six years after retiring. During his reign the Cornell teams won 29 IC4A championships, and perhaps his most famous pupil was John Paul Jones, the first IAAF mile record holder.

Moakley was one of those responsible for the US college system which produced so many top-class athletes. The college boys were heavily coached, trained hard and raced frequently – as we've seen through the stories of athletes such as Wes Santee – so it's interesting that one of the talents Moakley was most impressed by was the Briton Arnold Jackson, featured elsewhere on these pages as an Olympic star... and famously not a heavy trainer.

The only piece of technical running coaching Jackson had apparently been given was to cultivate a longer stride, and this virtually uncoached Olympic champion was the subject when Moakley said: "Give me that boy and I'd have what I always wanted, the four-minute mile."

ABOVE: Legendary American coach Jack Moakley held the top post at Cornell for five decades from 1899.

BELOW: Joe Binks had a 'cavalier' attitude to training. In later life this talented runner became a writer for the *News of the World*, and is pictured (rear) with British athletes and officials, including Roger Bannister, as Britain's team flew to Oslo.

However, ask many people to name one of the earliest coaches, and a London-born man of Arab, Turkish, French and Italian descent, named seemingly in honour of a Roman general who defeated Hannibal, and who featured prominently in the film Chariots of Fire could be a name which crops up.

Scipio Africanus 'Sam' Mussabini was a professional coach in an amateur era, and is best known now for his work with Harold Abrahams, but who has gone down in history as the only coach to have trained the winners of both the Olympic 100 and 1500 metre titles.

Born in 1867, Mussabini was, among many things, a professional sprinter, journalist and former cycling coach who had taken charge of Dunlop's cycle squad. Equally keen on athletics he coached South Africa's Reggie Watson to gold in the 1908 Olympics' 100 metres final, was successful again with his athletes at the 1912 games, and that same year became coach at the Polytechnic Harriers athletic club, a position he held for 15 years.

Elsewhere in this publication we mention the Chariots of Fire Paris Olympic Games, but Mussabini's influence is massive when it comes to the mile, not just because of his techniques, remarkable enough, but for who he would work with.

Those techniques included using the photographic influence of Eadweard Muybridge, the English photographer who studied motion. Mussabini bought his own camera and tripod to film runners and then played back the sequences to help improve stride pattern, starting technique and the dip finish. He helped sprinters, but then also used his analytical approach to aid longer distance runners too, most famously Albert Hill, who was mentioned in chapter five, and who provides a vital link through to Bannister and the eventual cracking of the four minute target.

Mussabini – as might be expected from a journalist – was a great source of quotes, the Bill Shankly of his day perhaps, and famously said: "Only think of two things – the gun and the tape. When you hear the one, just run like hell until you break the other."

But he was far more scientific than that may suggest and for those longer distances he had other methods and thoughts. He said: "Good running means easy running. There is no surer way of putting the brake on yourself and retarding progress than by straining and struggling with every nerve and muscle at full stretch."

He believed that every athlete had a 'speed limit' and the athlete had to learn what theirs was per lap. This was influenced by their running style, and the better the style the less energy expended.

Albert Hill had been a talented athlete but had never pursued his talent to the utmost, winning the AAA's four mile title in 1910, but then not competing in the championships for two years and not being considered for the 1912 Olympics.

The decisive moment in Hill's athletic career came in December 1912 when he joined Mussabini's Polytechnic Harriers. The coach quickly recognised the athlete's potential and the pair targeted the upcoming 1916 Berlin Olympics.

They worked on three areas, Hill's running style, his mental preparation and the ability to run at an even pace... something which the great Nurmi continued decades later.

His style became known as the 'poly swing' and saw him holding his arms lower and close to the body, swinging from the elbows, while the feet and knees were also low as possible as he ran, meaning a real economy of effort. The mental approach is illustrated well in Chariots of Fire, as the Mussabini character, played by Ian Holm, gathers information on the

RIGHT: Peter Snell was one of a host of athletes who reached the top thanks to coach Arthur Lydiard (right). Even today the coach's methods are influential, being founded on a strong endurance base and periodisation.

opposition, their style, strengths and weaknesses, and persuade his athletes that those opponents are beatable. Albert Hill was famously so relaxed before major races that he would fall asleep.

The final part of the jigsaw, the even pace, saw something which Nurmi would do years later, only for Hill it was the coach rather than the athlete holding a stopwatch during training and races. It would be used to help Hill run a race evenly, much against the 'fashion' of the day when the race would start in a cloud of dust, then see athletes ease up before engaging in a frenetic sprint for the line. Mussabini realised maintaining an even speed was far more efficient and would produce better performances.

By 1914 Hill was impressing at the AAA championships, but with the coming of the First World War, one of the potentially great careers in athletics was in danger of never reaching its full potential.

After the conflict the pair were reunited, Hill was famously triumphant at the 1920 Olympics at the age of 31, and went on to break the British mile record, advised by Mussabini, and also Walter George.

Hill retired not long after that race and turned to coaching, first with Blackheath Harriers and then assisting his own mentor Mussabini. After time in the US he became chief coach at Polytechnic Harriers following Mussabini's death in 1927... and the link to Bannister really comes next, for Hill started to coach a young schoolboy in 1931 who would go on to hold the world mile record, and many believe would have broken the four minute barrier if the Second World War hadn't intervened.

Sydney Wooderson's great potential was developed slowly and by the end of that decade he was in fantastic shape and ready to dominate. The fact that his best mile time actually followed the war in a race against Andersson just shows the lost potential, but it was after the war that a young Roger Bannister was inspired by Wooderson.

As Bannister said: "He (Wooderson) was not in the same league, but he came up and challenged the world record holder on the last bend. The challenge was fought off, but there was a feeling of courage that he showed in tackling the Swede, who looked physically much stronger. But this exchange, this battle was, I think, the thing which led me to go on from simple running for pleasure to running with this target of records, Olympic Games and other events in mind. ➤

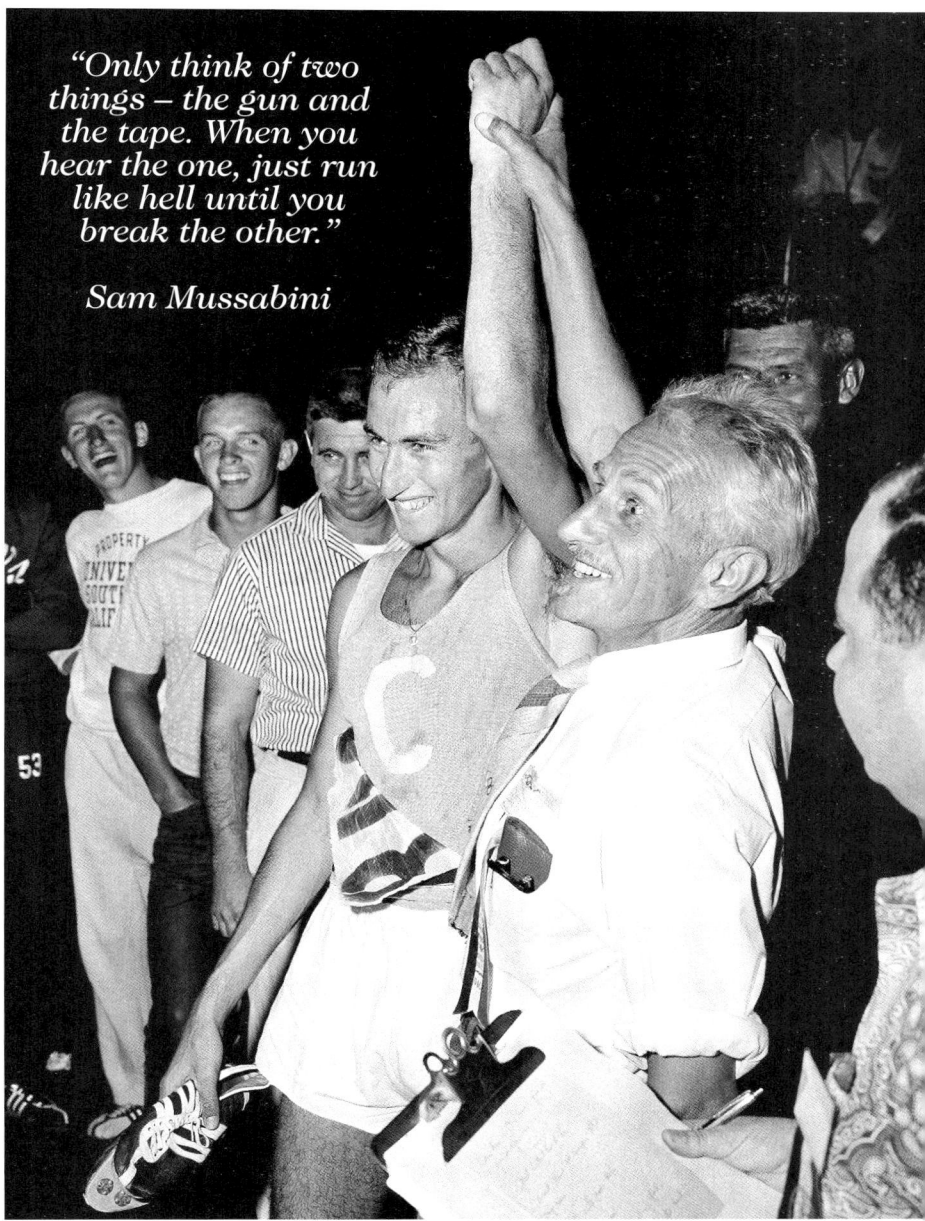

> "Only think of two things – the gun and the tape. When you hear the one, just run like hell until you break the other."
>
> Sam Mussabini

Coach Percy Cerutty with perhaps his greatest 'disciple', mile record holder Herb Elliott. Cerutty's methods were certainly considered strange for their time.

"The Swedes had had all the benefits of peace time during the war: better food, no rationing. He challenged them and ran very movingly. That, if you like, was the moment when I said, 'Well, that would be something I should like to do'."

The training methods of several other athletes – such as the Swedes before and during the Second World War and Paavo Nurmi – are mentioned elsewhere, but there are other influential names who deserve a mention before Bannister's own methods are examined, and they are two fierce rivals with opposing and contrasting methods.

Percy Cerutty, born near Melbourne, Australia, in 1895, has often been described as an eccentric, and his methods are described to some degree when the early career of John Landy is recorded.

Cerutty espoused what he called a 'Stotan' philosophy – a blend of stoic and Spartan thoughts and principles, and it involved a lot of running among the dunes of Victoria and a strict regime which meant no alcohol, no water or drink with meals or for a few hours after, no socialising late at night and no white bread. He certainly improved the times recorded by Landy, but that athlete's times were at their best in the period after he left Cerutty, while Herb Elliott could be the greatest of Cerutty's disciples with his spree of gold medals.

The Australian was firmly opposed to the interval training techniques supported by his great rival Franz Stampfl, who was born in Austria and fled Nazi-occupied Europe before the Second World War. Another great eccentric, Stampfl often wore a monocle and one former protégé said the first time he saw him Stampfl was washing his car trackside during an athletics event while wearing only Speedos.

Stampfl used many techniques to get the best from athletes over his long career – a career which continued even after an accident in 1980 left him a quadriplegic. Best known for espousing interval training, he was convinced a scientific approach was needed and devised a method in which athletes ran repeatedly over a set distance, however, each would be done at a faster speed than the one previous and the recovery period would become progressively shorter.

He began coaching Chris Brasher and it was he who introduced Chris Chataway and Roger Bannister to Stampfl in early 1954.

Chataway once said: "I am sure, under Franz, the three of us were fitter and better trained than before, but the main thing was his ability to invest it with magic."

But of course Bannister was already a world class athlete, one of the favourites to break the four minute barrier, and the medical man had his own methods.

"I suppose I was always independent," Bannister once said. "I felt about running that it was my task to find out what suited me and what didn't suit me, how much training could I do and then improve my performance, and not let my performance go down because I was training too hard. These were things which seemed to me so individual that nobody else was going to understand me to this degree.

"I had a common sense knowledge about what was needed. As a scientist, and I was a physiologist and did some research before I went on to my clinical training, trial and error. That's what science is. To me, running was an experiment. Here were muscles. Here was a heart. Here were lungs. To what extent can this bit of machinery be trained to do a very specific, skilled task?"

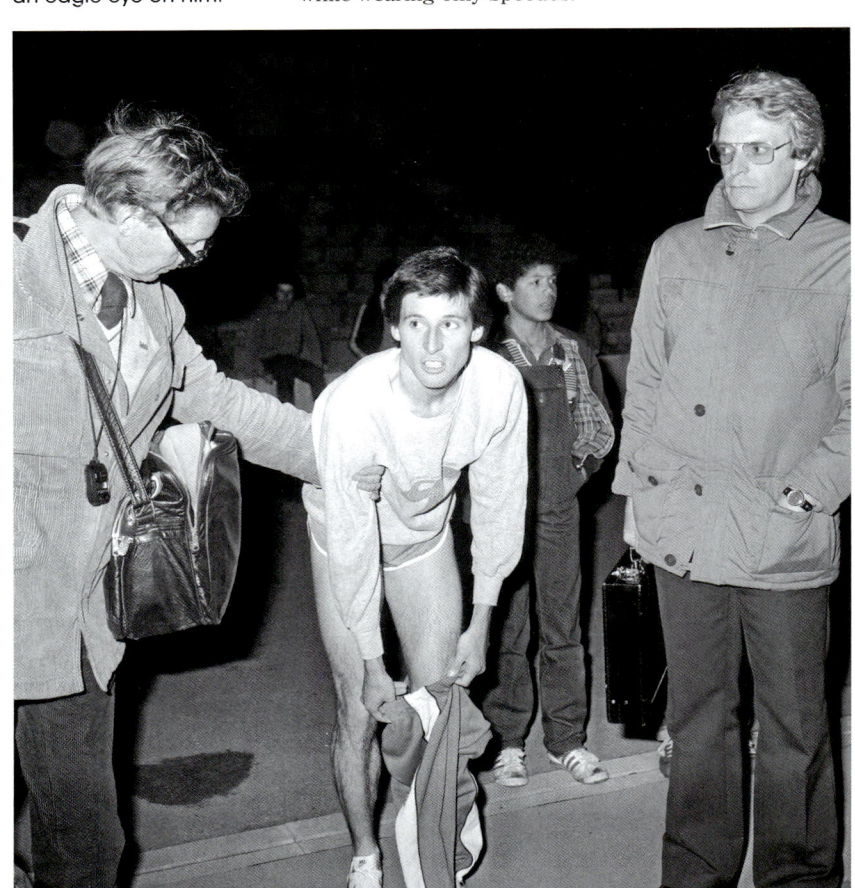

> *"I am sure, under Franz, the three of us were fitter and better trained than before, but the main thing was his ability to invest it with magic."*
>
> *Chris Chataway*

BELOW: Sebastian Coe made sure his training consisted of speed endurance, and it was his father Peter **(BELOW RIGHT)** who kept an eagle eye on him.

An examination of Bannister's training, recorded in his book The First Four Minutes, reveals just how compressed his preparations were. He ran between 30 and 45 miles a week and much of that took place at the Paddington track during his lunch hour when he was working at St Mary's Hospital.

As journalist John Goodbody reports in the spring 2014 edition of *Coaching Edge* magazine: "The standard session in the winter and spring of 1953/54 was 10 x 440 yards, with a two minute interval between each fast run, which gradually came down to 59 seconds per lap. In the final weeks before the record, he did two time trials over three-quarter miles, the last one of which was a solo 2 minutes 59.9 seconds, when he says he recovered quite quickly, and then, two days later, ran 880 yards 'quite easily' in 1 minute 52 seconds. He then had five days' rest before his feat at Oxford."

A comparison with Sebastian (now Lord) Coe is interesting and revealing, and something which Goodbody makes in his article.

Coe ran 50-70 miles a week, so considerably more than Bannister, and told Goodbody that most of it, under the guidance of his coach father, Peter, was "speed endurance and quality work. Fifty miles of that amount was either hard or very hard. Five to six days before I ran my world mile record of 3:47.33 seconds in 1981, I ran 6 x 800 metres, paced by a car, on undulating terrain but exactly measured, in one minute 51 seconds with one of them being one minute 46 seconds".

George Gandy, head endurance coach at Loughborough University and a student of the training techniques of his predecessors, points out some of the lessons learned over the years which have led to the record tumbling to current levels. And they are things which athletes like Albert Hill were also doing when it comes to relaxation and rest, while the interval methods of Stampfl, and even the 'whole person' philosophy of Cerutty comes into play too.

Gandy told Goodbody for his *Coaching Edge* article: "You have to live in the 'now'. I have said to Lisa Dobriskey (the world championships silver medallist) that she has to appreciate that in the Olympic final, her opponents are those who have qualified through the problems of life not just through the rounds of athletics. They are the toughest and most assertive fighters on the face of the planet and you have to face them. Therefore, you have to develop the skills of an assassin to complete the job.

"It is not just the actual running. The modern athlete has to have the correct lifestyle."

For Bannister, it was a personal quest, using his own scientific approach.

"I must be the international athlete who trained least," he said.

"I had worked out from my knowledge of physiology what was the minimum amount of training that would be needed to continue to improve year by year and every year. I would be reducing my mile best time by two or three seconds, you know, starting 4:18 and then gradually coming down. And basically I was doing interval training.

"I had so many other interests that I wanted to have my evenings free and I would usually miss lunch and sometimes there were rather unimportant lectures at 12 o'clock." ■

ABOVE: Roger Bannister had to fit his medical studies and work alongside his training, so he used his scientific mind to tackle the problem of using training time efficiently.

He's behind you...

ABOVE: Athletics' 'nearly man' John Landy was recovering from injury during his 'home' Olympics of 1956 and struggled to stay in touch as the pace quickened around the final bend.

John Landy… surely here was the man destined to be the one to break the four minute barrier? He had come so close, he had been knocking at the door. All he needed was some top-class competition… surely…

But human history is full of 'nearly' and 'if only'.

Just days before Roger Bannister finally ran under four minutes for the mile Landy had passed through London on his long journey from the southern hemisphere to Scandinavia and his attempt to make athletics history.

Bannister was near to the magic time, Santee was close, but Landy looked like the one to do it according to the form book and the cognoscenti. In all those fast races Down Under all he had lacked was serious competition to push him to fast times… and even so, he had run under 4:06 nine times since the 1952 Olympics. But did he truly believe?

As Bannister told he American Academy of Achievement in 2000: "The world record had been stopped for eight years, so there hadn't been any progress. That was why people said, 'well, maybe it can't be done. Is it a psychological or physical barrier?' But John Landy had run four minutes and two seconds the previous year. So had I, and so had an American runner (Santee). Gunder Haegg held the record. The Swedes weren't involved in the war and learned some techniques from the prewar Germans about how hard you could train and they put it to good effect. The war had set back our progress in Britain because nothing happened for four or five years."

Landy had targets. First up he wanted that sub-four run, and the 'perfect' conditions of Paavo Nurmi's homeland and quality opposition in Europe would surely be what was needed. Then after making history there were championships to win – notably the British Empire and Commonwealth Games (the name newly changed from the British Empire Games) starting at the end of July.

He left Melbourne on April 28, travelling via Singapore, Calcutta (now Kolkata), Karachi, Beirut and London before reaching Stockholm and then Turku, the birthplace of Nurmi, on May 3.

After such a long journey he acclimatised and began training… but within days he knew that the quest to be the first was over. News came from England that Bannister had beaten him with that 3:59.4.

So what now? Well, he could prove he was even faster then the Englishman, and he could still go for gold in Vancouver.

He started well in Finland and on May 31 he set a blistering pace and reached the bell two seconds ahead of Bannister's pace. However, he paid for the quick start and finished in 4:01.6, still a personal best time for the Australian. Then just eight days later he recorded exactly the same time.

Then, on June 21 at Turku, Landy kicked down the door which Bannister had opened.

With Chris Chataway – confident he could beat Landy – in the field alongside a number of good Finnish runners, conditions were perfect for a fast time. Local runner Aulis Kallio led through the first lap in 58.3, with Landy just 0.2 behind him, then the Australian took on the pace himself, passing 880 yards in 1:58.7.

But according to author and statistician Bob Phillips, it was what happened next which stunned the running world. "It was landy's third lap of 58.5 which ensured the record. This was revolutionary running. For half a century the third lap had been regarded as a necessary evil."

What Landy did was accelerate, and yet still Chataway would not be shaken, and as the bell was passed in 2:57.2 by the Aussie, the Briton was hot on his heels in 2:57.5. Landy rounded the bend and then poured on more pressure to finally break his opponent, passing the 1500 metre mark in 3:41.8 – a new world record – and then crossing the finish line 40 yards ahead in 3:57.9, which was then rounded up to 3:58.

Landy had finally broken through four minutes, and at the same time shattered Bannister's record by a significant margin.

The stage was set for Vancouver, and a showdown with Bannister.

To say there was excitement was an understatement. Norris McWhirter summed it up for readers of *Athletics World* when describing how it was a classic battle between two men of wildly contrasting styles – the man with the "most devastating finish of any miler" – after all, Bannister had recently run an average time in London, but with a final lap of 53.8 seconds – against the ➤

TOP: Ireland's Ron Delany took 1500 metres gold in Melbourne ahead of East Germany's Klaus Richtzenhain and then fast-finishing John Landy. It was another blow to the Australian, who had lost out to Roger Bannister two years earlier in the race for the first sub-four.

ABOVE: Former rivals, old friends, Roger Bannister and John Landy.

FOUR MINUTE MILE 69

"greatest pace runner ever seen" – Landy's third lap during his world record providing the evidence that the race might effectively be over before Bannister had a chance to employ his superb finishing burst. McWhirter had dubbed it the "Mile of the Millennium".

The first two men to break four minutes were going head to head, and the world's press was taking notice. The still relatively young medium of television was there to record proceeding and broadcast to millions across North America, while back in the UK and elsewhere in the Commonwealth, radios were tuned in.

There had been heats before the final, and the two were drawn apart for this stage. Bob Phillips describes how Landy's fellow Australian Geoff Warren seemingly tried to wear Bannister out by setting a fast pace in their heat, but the Englishman was sticking to his own plans and qualified comfortably in third place, while Landy won his heat but in a slower time.

In the meantime both were nursing fitness concerns, Bannister's following a cold, Landy a foot injury which had required stitches. However, Landy – known as one of the world's greatest sportsmen – always claimed it made no difference to his race.

Come the final, they were ready for only their second race against each other in four years, the previous one being a heat of the 1952 Olympic 1500 metres, and the race of contrasts began, the tall Englishman with the long stride against the shorter, more powerful Australian.

New Zealanders Murray Halberg and Bill Baillie took the race out, but Landy quickly took it on, passing the first 440 yards in 58.2, just five yards ahead of Bannister who was deciding to respond to the danger a long Landy lead could pose. The world record holder was running to form and type and really put an effort in over the next lap, stretching his advantage to as much as 12-13 yards, and at the half mile he was through in 1:58.2, compared with the Briton's 1:59.6.

In his book First Four Minutes, Bannister said: "This was when my confidence wavered. I quickened my stride, trying at the same time to keep relaxed. I was almost hypnotised by his easy shuffling stride – the most clipped and economical I have ever seen. I tried to imagine myself attached to him by some invisible cord. With each stride I drew the cord tighter and reduced his lead."

Landy maintained his pace, and recorded a third lap of 60.2, but this time it was Bannister who had proven that the third lap was crucial, and this time in a race rather than a record attempt, as he scorched round nearly a second faster than the Australian and was nearly on his shoulder at the bell.

Landy accelerated again down the back straight, opening up a gap, but again Bannister closed as they rounded the last bend.

Bannister later said: "If Landy did not slacken soon I would be finished. As we entered the last bend I tried to convince myself that he was tiring. With each stride now I attempted to husband a little strength for the moment at the end of the bend when I had decided to pounce.

"I knew this would be the point he would least expect me, and if I failed to overtake him the race would be his."

And it's this point which would go down in athletics folklore, as going into the home straight Landy looked back to his left at the exact same moment Bannister went past on his right.

"I flung myself past Landy," Bannister said. "As I did so I saw him glance inwards over his opposite shoulder. This tiny act of his held great significance and gave me confidence."

A bronze sculpture of the two men at this moment was created by Vancouver sculptor Jack Harman in 1967 from a photo by photographer Charlie Warner, and even now reminds tourists of one of sport's defining images.

Bannister held his form and reached the line first in a time of 3:58.8 – as usual by now collapsing into the arms of an official – with Landy in second, with a time of 3:59.6.

As Landy wrote later: "I was by nature a front runner and with my very limited international experience I felt I had no option but to run in front in Vancouver.

"I felt the way to win the race was to start out running a fairly fast half, then pour on a very hard third quarter and then keep going to beyond the point where traditionally Bannister began his 300 metres sprint. I thought if I kept that going, even if I eventually slowed

> *"I flung myself past Landy. I saw him glance inwards over his opposite shoulder. This tiny act held great significance and gave me confidence."*

BELOW: The first mile race in history in which two runners finished under four minutes saw Roger Bannister cross the line ahead of John Landy at the British Empire Games in Vancouver on August 7, 1954. Bannister stopped the watch at 3:58.8, Landy finished in 3:59.6.

down, I might break him and once I'd got clear he'd never catch up.

"When I got to the last bend, the angle of the sun had changed and I had lost Bannister's shadow. I thought that I might have shaken him off. That's when I looked over my shoulder. I looked left and not right because I was looking for confirmation that he was about 10 or 15 metres behind me. In fact, he was right behind me. I turned but it was too late. People said looking round cost me the race, but that isn't true. I was absolutely leaden legged, I'd really given it everything I had."

The fast finisher, the race runner, had beaten the front runner, and it was chaos at the finish as the other runners attempted to cross the line.

Bannister was full of praise for his opponent, a man he clearly respected and admired: "He is the sort of runner I could never become. Before Vancouver he achieved a record of solo mile races that I could never have equalled. At Vancouver he had the courage to lead at the same speed in a closely competitive race. His boldness forced me to abandon my time schedule and lose myself quite completely in the struggle itself."

The world record holder was equal in his sportsmanship, saying: "I tried to set a fast pace from the start. I did exactly as I wanted, but I was beaten by a better man today."

Years later, he would say: "I don't have the temperament of a race winner. I just like to run fast."

For Bannister it was nearly the end, with just one quality epilogue to come for the man who had been so disappointed at the 1952 Olympics, and who had set himself three targets – the sub-four, Commonwealth victory, and European 1500 metres gold.

At Berne in the Europeans he achieved his ambition, beating a host of good runners, and once again scorching a final lap of 54.7 to take that title.

Then it was a well-earned retirement from athletics, and a long and illustrious medical career. ➤

ABOVE: England's golden boy – Roger Bannister finally took the gold medal he had craved when he won the 'Mile of the Century' at the Empire Games in Vancouver. John Landy was second and Richard Ferguson of Canada, right, was third.

LANDY... THE ULTIMATE SPORTING GENTLEMAN

For readers of a certain generation, the name Alf Tupper will have resonance. He was the cartoon hero of 1950s comic books such as The Rover and The Victor and was known as Tough of the Track... a working class athletics hero who would rescue people on his way to an athletics meet and still win despite turning up late, who would work all night and fall asleep on the bus to the track, or who would be tripped mid-race ... yet go on to win.

Well John Landy brought Alf Tupper to life, and in any list of 'great sporting moments' – and in the true sense of the word sporting – he is usually somewhere near the summit.

As much as for his distinguished record-breaking career, in his native Australia Landy is often best remembered for his performance in the 1500 metres final at the 1956 Australian National Championships.

In that race, and while on world record pace, Landy stopped and doubled back to check on the young Ron Clarke after Clarke's heel had been clipped, causing him to fall early in the third lap of the race... the point at which Landy usually poured on the speed and made his move. Landy hadn't caused the fall, but he 'spiked' Clarke as he attempted to avoid the fallen man.

Clarke, at that time the junior 1500 metre world champion, got back to his feet and started running again; Landy did similar, raced past Clarke... and went for it.

With the rest of the field 30 or 40 yards away Landy made up the gap... and won.

If you really don't believe it, log on to a popular video website and search for 'John Landy Stops to Help Fallen Ron Clarke'.

It was typical of the man, and staggered those who witnessed it. One of those, Dr Gordon Moyes, said: "Landy... did the most incredibly stupid, beautiful, foolish, gentlemanly act I have ever seen. He stopped, ran back to the fallen young Ron Clarke and helped him up to his feet, brushed cinders from knees, and checking his bloodied shoulder said, 'sorry'."

Harry Gordon, in the Melbourne Sun, wrote: "In a nutshell, you sacrificed your chance of a world record to go to the aid of a fallen rival. And in pulling up, trotting back to Ron Clarke, muttering 'sorry' and deciding to chase the field you achieved much more than any world record.

"It was a senseless piece of chivalry, but it will be remembered as one of the finest actions in the history of sport."

Looking at the bare statistics, athletics fans can't help but wonder what could have been. Landy was on top form and won the race just six seconds outside the world record.

He later said: "I stopped involuntarily and for a moment I thought, I've been disqualified. Then I thought, no, I'm still in the race. It looked impossible, with the rest of the field some 30 yards ahead, but I thought I'd better have a go. I was in a blind panic, and I didn't think about times or tactics. I just ran."

John Landy's sporting action in helping Ron Clarke to his feet and then winning the race gained many awards. Here Jack Crump, secretary of Britain's Amateur Athletic Association, presents one such memento.

John Landy's tactic in Vancouver had been to try and run the 'kick' out of Roger Bannister by pushing the pace... and it almost worked.

For Landy, there were a few more chapters in a remarkable story, including one which would mark this gentleman of the track as one of the great sportsmen, as well as a man who would be forever frustrated at the major championships.

The next Olympics were due to be held in Australia, and that was a massive incentive for him to continue racing despite the start of his teaching career.

Some very quick early season races during his build up to the Olympic year proved he would be in contention should his fitness hold, and two mile races of 3:58.6 confirmed this.

In the Olympic trials he stunned the world by winning after stopping to help the young Ron Clarke – see the separate story. The incident is still talked about six decades on as an example of his sportsmanship and fair play.

However, with the games just around the corner, the 'poster boy' of the Melbourne games – the first Olympics to be held in the southern hemisphere – embarked on an American tour, and it was there that he injured his Achilles tendon. He continued to train but the injury failed to clear and his chances of competing, let alone winning a medal, were in doubt.

By the end of October, and just over three weeks from the November 22 opening ceremony, he said that he was fit to run… but that he was not expecting to be 100%.

Landy qualified for the final of the 1500 metres and in that race he started slowly… which for his style of running and racing was very different, and could land him in trouble against the likes of Irishman Ron Delany, Germany's Klaus Richtzenhain, Briton Brian Hewson and Hungarian Laszlo Tabori. The early pace was fairly pedestrian, but when the race exploded into action on the third lap Landy was forced to run wide, and with his Achilles injury perhaps on his mind he didn't push on as instinct may have told him to.

Delany stormed away to win with Landy fighting until the end and clinching third.

He later said: "I thought I had no chance at all before the race. Only in the last straight did I begin to hope."

Roger Bannister, by this time covering the event for Sports Illustrated magazine, said: "I believe Landy could have won. But he ran as though he knew he could not win. For Landy this was probably the end of the greatest solo mile-running career the world has seen and of an athlete faster, neater and more generous than any other."

Landy retired from athletics… but this great sportsman would remain in the public eye in his homeland. A passionate conservationist and naturalist, this 'everyman' from Down Under displayed the best in sporting attributes, and went on to become the 25th governor of the state of Victoria. ∎

ABOVE: John Landy, right, took the crowd's applause along with fellow Australian greats Ron Clarke and Marjorie Jackson-Nelson at 2006's Commonwealth Games.

After the event

For Roger Bannister, life was never going to be the same once he'd broken the four minute barrier for the mile. The realist that he was, Bannister knew the time itself would be beaten – indeed until the remarkable Ovett versus Coe record blitz in the early 1980s, his possession of the record time was the shortest in the IAAF era.

But his claiming of the record will always be the most famous. What will never be beaten is the fact that he was the first to do it. He was the sporting equivalent of astronaut Neil Armstrong, or climber Edmund Hillary or explorer Matthew Flinders.

He had been to places and done things first, and the danger after that, of course, is that you can forever be known as 'didn't you', for past achievements rather than any future ambitions... 'didn't you break the four minute mile?'

That was never a danger with Bannister. For him athletics was only ever going to be an interlude, and five decades after the 1954 feat, at the end of an interview with the BBC, he was asked whether the sub-four minute mile was his most important achievement. His reply was that no, it wasn't. His medical career, and also the contribution to sports administration he made, were far more significant.

What he had to accept was that the whirlwind which ensued during the rest of 1954 was always going to change his life, and perhaps opened doors which may not have been available to him normally.

Of course Bannister nearly never went for that sub-four... not because he couldn't, but because if he'd won gold at the Olympics of 1952, his studies and career would have then taken over as his sporting ambition at that time would have been achieved. But famously, and as described earlier, men's 1500 metres Olympic gold in 1952 was not destined for Britain. ➤

TOP LEFT: Peerless and Matchless – Roger Bannister aboard an Army Matchless G3/L motorcycle. He became a recognisable face and a good recruiting sergeant!

FAR LEFT & LEFT: The social whirl continued for Bannister after breaking the record, and honours came too. He is pictured with Queen Elizabeth in 1956, and outside Buckingham Palace with his wife Moyra and his mother in 1955 after being made a CBE.

BELOW LEFT: A year after their run Chataway, Brasher and Bannister inspected a plaque at the Iffley Road track.

BELOW: Harold Abrahams presented Bannister with the Helms Trophy, an award which recognised outstanding achievement.

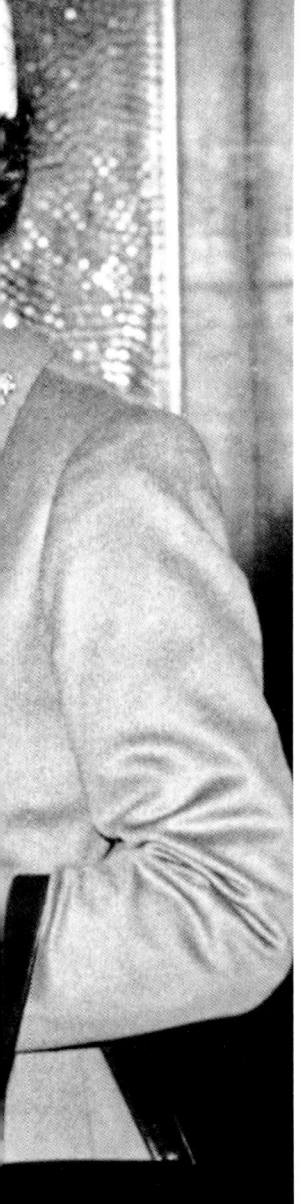

FOUR MINUTE MILE 75

RIGHT: Roger Bannister was determined that medicine would be his life, but his fellow medical students at St Mary's Hospital in Paddington, London were nevertheless proud of their colleague.

BELOW RIGHT: Bannister had many roles to play after his athletics career, and was pictured here, along with his wife Moyra, with Prime Minister Margaret Thatcher and husband Denis at a Downing Street reception.

BELOW: As a busy surgeon and chairman of the Sports Council, it may have been tricky to find time for the family, but the photographers were allowed in to see the Bannisters playing football in their garden.

BELOW RIGHT: The achievements of 1954 have been immortalised on screen, a 2005 version seeing actor Jamie Maclachlan as Bannister.

FAR RIGHT: Bannister, Chataway and Brasher were often reunited on the anniversaries of the record run. In the top picture the three marked the 40th anniversary, while in 1974 they were snapped jogging down Portland Place to the BBC, where they featured in a programme to mark their achievement.

As Bannister said: "If I had won the gold medal, I would probably have retired because Olympic gold medals, 1500 metres, there was nothing higher and I would just have gone on with my work. But I felt angry with the press, angry at myself, angry with the organisers of the event and thought about it.

"I knew that I could go on for two more years when the equivalent of an Olympic prize would have been the European championships and the Commonwealth (Empire) games. So after thought, I decided it would be possible to work and go on training. It proved difficult."

Then once the four-minute barrier was reached, and the other targets of 1954 – including that defeat of Landy in the Empire Games – it was over, but not before a host of events and awards.

Bannister met top politicians, royalty and celebrities – he would never consider himself one of those, yet was conscious that his senior colleagues may not be amused if he was at a London cocktail party instead of at the hospital where his 'real' work was.

Earlier in 1954, Bannister had met Moyra Jacobsson, daughter of a former head of the International Monetary Fund – contrary to movie versions of their life, which had them meeting earlier in the decade. The pair eventually married in 1955, and went on to have four children.

Lord Bill Deedes reported how: "The Foreign Office wanted Bannister to make a trip to America. They thought it would improve Anglo-American relations and show the United States what Britain could do. Back in 1954, we were still trying to convince the world that the depredations of the Second World War hadn't written us off."

Of course the problem was that this was verging on the 'professional' – the very thing of which great athletes of the recent past had fallen foul. 'Expenses' as stipulated by the IAAF were limited at £12, so the political minefield of sports administration was very much in Bannister's conscience. Deedes described how Bannister had to refuse a gold Miracle Mile Trophy, as it was valued at £178... way beyond that £12 mark.

But for the man himself, it was all taken in that long, raking stride.

After retiring from athletics, medicine became the primary focus, but there were other activities too, including writing for the *Sunday Times* and for publications in the United States, as well as writing a book on running.

He certainly knew the next phase of his life would be difficult, or interesting at the very least. A fiercely intelligent man, he knew his would be the name on everyone's lips, but that he was 'bottom of the pile' when it came to medicine... his reputation on the track meant for nothing in that environment, and he had to work.

"My colleagues and my teachers, of course, had some difficulties in dealing with me because I was famous, notorious, infamous – whichever phrase you like to use. And the concept that I could also have a serious career, and indeed in a very highly competitive field like neurology, was really rather strange to them. There were those who supported me, but I certainly felt I was being examined rather carefully," he said.

In an interview in 2000, he said: "My core, my whole life, was medicine. I wanted to become a specialist. So for 10 years I concentrated solely on medicine. It took 10 years to become a consultant in neurology." ➤

The young doctor did his national service in the army – always a good photo opportunity for Her Majesty's forces – and worked hard. But his profile always meant he could open influential doors too.

"I was asked to be the chairman of the Sports Council, and that has really been the pattern since. Alongside my neurology, I have always had some public involvement in sports and sports promotion."

Sport was and is something Bannister always pushed as a great benefit to youngsters.

"To be effective, exercise should become a habit and like other habits is best learnt in childhood. Some children do find competitive sport difficult. But even if pupils lack the skills to succeed in sport, life itself brings reverses. Sport is a way of learning to accept them with grace."

That Sports Council role lasted from 1971 to 1974, at a time when major projects were followed through and sports centres sprang up across the UK, and he also helped develop a test to determine whether athletes had taken anabolic steroids (with Canadian Ben Johnson the most high-profile 'victim' exposed). As a leading neurologist he conducted research into diseases of the autonomic nervous system, his being a definitive textbook on the subject.

He had been awarded the CBE in 1955, and 20 years later was knighted, not for his sporting achievements, but perhaps more satisfying to the man himself for his services to medicine. That same year, 1975, he was involved in a car accident, badly hurting his ankle. A decade after that he became Master of Oxford's Pembroke College, a post he held until 1993.

But this year, perhaps above all others, interest has been rekindled in one of the great sporting achievements in history, which still has resonance, and the 85-year-old Bannister is again at the centre. So he is once again using his position to benefit others, this time by acting as patron of the 2014 Bupa Westminster Mile on May 24, an event billed as the world's biggest timed road mile of 2014. ➤

TOP: Bannister and Chataway scooped two top awards in 1954. Bannister was named Sportsman of the Year by the *Sporting Record*, while Chataway was the first man to win BBC Sports Personality.

ABOVE: Always happy to give interviews when possible, Bannister was pictured here while talking to The Associated Press in 2012.

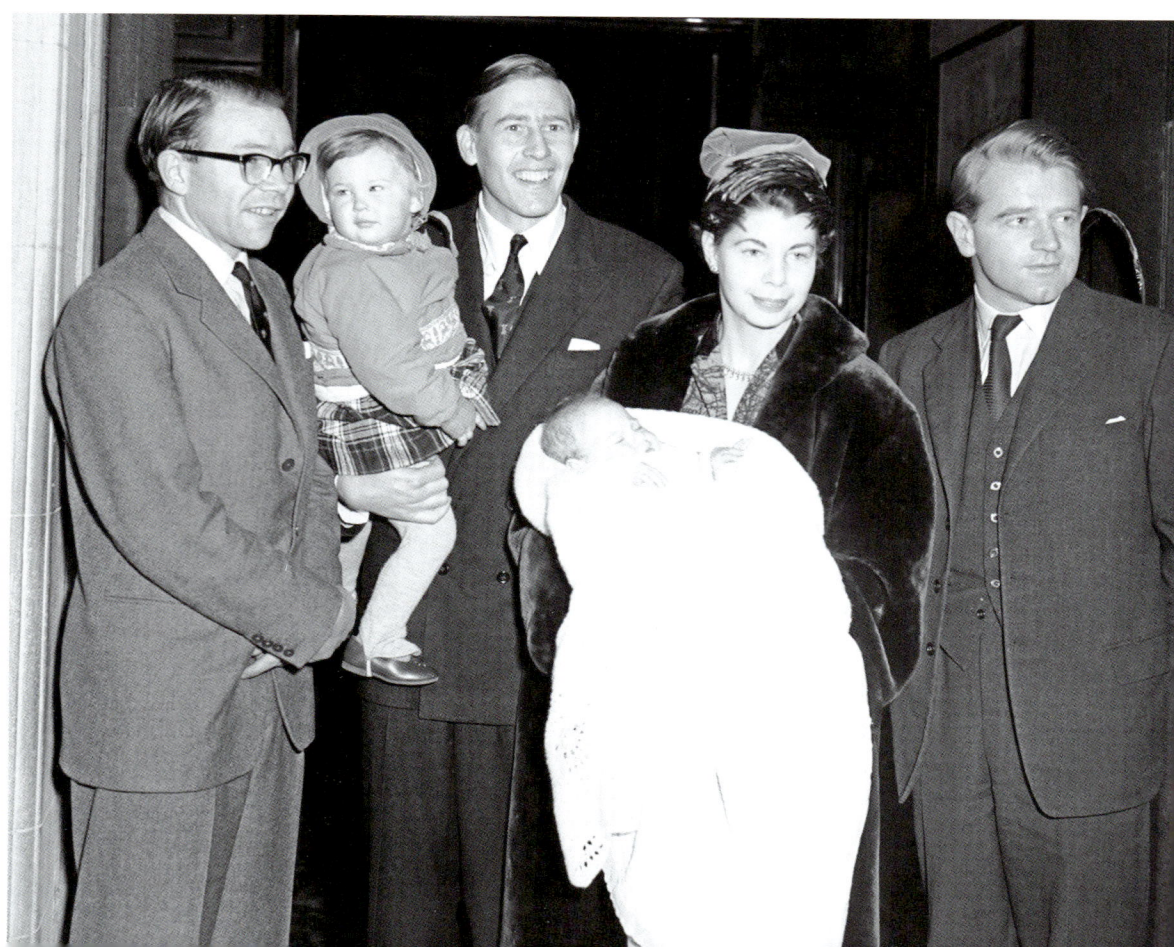

RIGHT: The Bannisters were headline news, and the press were there at the christening of Clive Christopher Roger in 1959. Here Roger holds two-year-old daughter Erin, Moyra shows off young Clive, while the two godfathers Brasher and Chataway complete the happy picture.

LEFT: Roger Bannister wore his chairman of the Sports Council 'hat' when seeing plans for development at Chelsea football club with chairman Brian Mears, manager Dave Sexton and architect John Darbourne in 1972.

BELOW LEFT: The Bannisters were guests of honour at the Westminster Mile in 2006.

BELOW: Brunel University presented Dr Roger Bannister with an honorary degree in 2008.

FOUR MINUTE MILE 79

ABOVE: Feted and honoured, Sir Roger Bannister was central to the London 2012 celebrations and held aloft the Olympic Flame when it visited the Iffley Road Stadium in Oxford that July.

ABOVE RIGHT: Medical recognition is just as important to Bannister. Here he holds a lifetime achievement award from the American Academy of Neurology.

RIGHT: Fellow mile record holder and London 2012 organiser Sebastian Coe walked the track with Bannister in Oxford.

80 FOUR MINUTE MILE

RIGHT: Enjoying meeting a new generation, Bannister chatted and laughed with children from Our Lady's school in Poplar during a Sport Relief event.

BELOW: Bannister and Diane Charles (Leather) helped launch the publicity for the 2014 Westminster Mile, which would celebrate their achievements of six decades ago.

BOTTOM: Bannister and The Queen started the Commonwealth baton relay for the 2002 Manchester games.

At the publicity events to announce the Westminster Mile, Bannister said he was flattered by the interest in his achievements six decades ago: "I have been astonished. If it brings other people in to running then it is all for the good and I am still very happy to do all I can to help.

"I myself was inspired after being taken to see Sydney Wooderson and I realised that was the sport I wanted to do. It happens to be the centenary of the birth of Sydney, who I saw challenging the Swedes, who had been the record holders during the war.

"There may be many children, of all different age groups, who can be inspired. It made all the difference to me and all of the athletes I ran with and ran against – they were inspired by the previous generation so it all locks together."

As for the future of the mile world record, which at time of writing belongs to Hicham El Guerrouj at 3:43.13, Bannister has said before that there may well be a physical barrier, but doesn't think it's been reached yet.

"I think it will go on being broken until it gets down to 3:30. Since I did it, it has gone down a third of a second a year, on average. It is now down to 3:43. But, without cheating with drugs, I don't think anyone will ever beat 3:30." ∎

The race is over...
but records
tumble

It's one of the great pub quiz questions: Who ran the first four minute mile? Answering too quickly and without thinking, the typical contestant will say 'Roger Bannister'... but of course every youngster is told to listen to a question properly, and if you do that, it's a very different answer, and a name which features large in the era after the feats of Iffley Road, Vancouver or Berne.

On September 3, 1958, more than four years after Bannister's first sub-four minute mile, Derek Ibbotson finished fourth in a race at London's White City which was won by the prodigious talent Herb Elliott, the young Australian. The victor crossed the line in 3:55.4, but 'Ibbo' as he was popularly known, finished in 4:00.0.

But that has stepped forward in time a bit too much, and for the purposes of this publication we need to rewind slightly. This isn't a complete history of middle distance running or indeed of British middle distance running, so fans of Gordon Pirie shouldn't feel that their hero is being ignored, although he was a fierce competitor and the first winner of the Emsley Carr Mile, a race instigated by Sir William Carr and named after his father Sir Emsley, a former editor of the News of the World.

The annual race began in 1953 and was aimed at helping athletes break the four minute 'barrier'. By the time of the second event, that record had already been shattered.

That first Emsley Carr race had been billed as an effort by the highly-rated American Wes Santee to show the Europeans what he could do and that he was a threat to the sub-four, but it was Pirie, better known for cross country and longer track distances, who stepped down in distance to help improve his speed... and who beat Santee.

Pirie was a good miler but definitely a great athlete, defeating such legends of the sport as Emil Zatopek and Vladimir Kuts. Hard as nails and dedicated in his preparation, he often ran 200 miles or more per week in training and in 1955 was named at the second BBC Sports Personality of the Year. In 1965 readers of Athletics Weekly voted Pirie as their greatest ever British athlete, with 36% voting for him ahead of Roger Bannister on 19%.

Winner of the Emsley Carr Mile in Olympic year, 1956, was Ibbotson, but he was entered in the 5000 metres in Melbourne and instead the 1500 metres Down Under was the first major championship since that momentous year of 1954 and the Bannister versus Landy battles. The Australian went in as mile record holder, while also in the frame were Jim Bailey, Gunnar Nielsen, Laszlo Tabori and Istvan Rozsavolgyi, as well as a young Irishman, Ron Delany. He had come to prominence two years earlier in the European Championships' 800 metres when aged just 19, now as a college runner in the US for Villanova, Delany was battle hardened and trained to a peak, his college coach often pushing him to 10 x 440 yards in less than 60 seconds each. ▶

ABOVE: Derek Ibbotson became the ninth man to break the four minute mile when he won the Emsley Carr Mile in 1956. A year later he lowered the mile record.

ABOVE LEFT: Ibbotson was made an MBE by The Queen in 2008.

FAR LEFT: Grit Briton... imagine Coe and Ovett battling in conditions like this? Ibbotson was the epitome of the battling athlete, as shown in this picture from a race at White City against Chris Chataway.

LEFT: Ibbotson never 'left anything on the track', giving his all each time he ran. Here in 1962 he crosses the line first in a mile race at Blackpool.

ABOVE RIGHT: Australia's Herb Elliott dominated the 1500 metres in the 1960 Olympics, here leading Hungary's Istvan Rozsavolgyi, France's Michel Jazy, Romania's Zoltan Varnos and Frenchman Michel Bernard, on his way to a world record 3:35.6.

ABOVE & BELOW: The personable Elliott after winning at Cardiff's Empire Games in 1958. After athletics he enjoyed a long and successful business career.

RIGHT: Elliott went four years without losing a mile or 1500 metres race.

Delany took the Olympics 1500 title in 3:41.2, scorching round the last lap in 54 seconds, and had a good couple of seasons in the mile, recording 3:58.8 in 1957 and 3:57.5 in 1958. At the Rome Olympics he was disappointing, then he retired from the sport, but not before inspiring a generation of Irish runners, including one who would earn the nickname of the 'Chairman of the Boards', and who adds his insight later in this publication.

But it was Ibbotson who was the enigma. At Melbourne Roger Bannister had presented his, by now, nine fellow members of the sub-four club with a black silk tie emblazoned with a silver '4' and golden 'MM', and Ibbotson was one of those, as his time winning that Emsley Carr had equalled Bannister's 3:59.4 and according to journalist and statistician Bob Phillips, 'Ibbo' had only entered to sharpen his speed... and also to get an extra ticket for the post meeting banquet! Delany was one of those he had well beaten.

Ibbotson was a popular character with the fans and the press back in the UK, and ran a lot of races... often approaching 70 per season, a schedule which many experts believe prevented him from reaching his true potential. Born in 1932 in Huddersfield, West Yorkshire, he was an excellent junior, and when he went into the RAF for his national service his athletic abilities were encouraged.

"Out of the corner of my eye I saw Lewandowski moving up. Delany and Wood couldn't be far behind. Fear gave me wings."

In 1956 at Melbourne he took bronze in the 5000 but that 'warm-up' mile had influenced which direction his running would take, and he focused on the shorter distance for the following season – as many 5000 metre men would to sharpen up and build their leg speed, racing at a faster pace than they would need for longer distances.

In July 1957 his moment of athletics immortality arrived. He felt in good shape, and targeted a 3:57, asking fellow competitor Mike Blagrove if he would set a pace of 1:57 or just under for the half mile. These were heady days, because on the 11th of that month Finland's Olavi Salsola broke the world 1500 metres record, only for Stanislav Jungwirth of Czechoslovakia to knock two seconds off that time the very next day. Ibbotson's attempt on the mile mark came just seven days after that second race and was at London's White City, with Delany, Jungwirth, Ken Wood and Stansislaw Lewandowski also in the field... so such ambitious 'pacemaking' was par for the course in such record-breaking days.

Blagrove went out quickly, perhaps too quickly, but by the halfway point was pretty much on the schedule Ibbotson had hoped for, 1:55.8. Jungwirth took the race on as Blagrove tired with Ibbotson close behind. Bob Phillips records Ibbotson's thoughts at the time in his book, 3:59.4: The Quest for the Four Minute Mile, as: "Jungwirth looked tremendously strong and seemed he could go on indefinitely."

What the Czech was thinking and how he really felt wasn't known to Ibbotson, all he could control were his own actions, and the Yorkshireman says those actions were actually prompted by a fear that the others were massing to overtake.

"Out of the corner of my right eye I saw Lewandowski moving up. Delany and Wood could not be far behind. It was the moment of truth. Fear gave me wings," he said. Ibbotson went for it, leaving a world class field in his wake. Neil Allen of *The Times* described Ibbotson's win, in a time of 3:57.2, as the greatest in modern middle distance running and better than

84 FOUR MINUTE MILE

LEFT & BELOW: Peter Snell was on a golden run of form in the early 1960s. The picture left shows him beating Belgium's Roger Moens to seal Olympic gold in Tokyo, while below he held off George Kerr of Jamaica at the Empire Games of 1962.

Bannister's defeat of Landy in the Empire Games of 1954. The Olympic champions and world record holders were defeated and floundering in his wake, and the first four men across the line were under four minutes.

Fans of Delany say he was boxed in at a crucial point of that final lap and, given a clear run, would – or could – have won and taken the record himself. He actually finished second. But of course this was a race, tactics and manoeuvres were always a part of it and pacemaking was frowned upon… even at the White City event one British official refused to sign off the time as a world record because of the agreed pacing by Blagrove.

Luckily for Ibbotson the IAAF saw fit to ratify the time as a new world best.

The record was shifting onwards at an inexorable rate, and more and more men were dipping under the old 'barrier'. That same year yet more athletes recorded times better than the four minute mark, including Don Bowden – the first American to run under the time in 3:58.7 – Merv Lincoln from Australia, Sweden's Dan Waern and the Belgian 800 metres world record holder Roger Moens.

Many still didn't see Ibbotson as a 'natural' miler, believing him better at the longer track distances, but perhaps above anything else he was a racer, a competitor. It's often said this was his undoing, that once he took that mile world record (and a place among sport's elite club) he remained at the distance instead of concentrating on his 'natural' distance of perhaps 5000 metres, and also cutting down his schedule.

The criticism Ibbotson often faces is that he burned out, but he had always worked hard, trained hard and raced often.

Ibbotson simply never quite recaptured that form, but he was also one of many athletes who were simply blown away by the next phenomenon to hit the sport… a young Australian whose career blazed brightly, then was over, with many still considering him the greatest middle distance runner of them all and who exercised such authority over the middle distances.

Herb Elliott, born in Perth in 1938, was a teenage prodigy, and was described by his fellow countryman John Landy as perhaps the greatest natural talent he had ever seen. Already a very talented junior, he was ➤

taken by his family to watch the 1956 Olympic Games in Melbourne and decided to stay in that city to work with renowned coach Percy Cerutty. As Elliott said, he would "do some hard training for the first time in my life".

As already described, Cerutty could perhaps best be described as eccentric, but he was certainly effective in turning our top class runners, using his 'Stotan' philosophy – his unique combination of Spartan and stoic methods – to forge a generation of athletes.

Elliott lived in a cramped bunk-house at the coach's Portsea training centre, training among the sand dunes, lifting weights, and absorbing the style and Cerutty 'brand' of coaching, a style which Landy and fellow track distance star Ron Clarke didn't enjoy.

But Elliott seemed the perfect pupil. "I have never seen a young man with greater determination or a greater capacity for self-punishment," said his coach.

The transformation in Elliott was amazing, whether it was purely down to Cerutty's methods, or the athlete simply maturing, the times tumbled. On January 12, 1957, Elliott ran the mile in 4:06, a junior world best, and later won the Victoria Championships in the same time, before recording a 880 yard junior world record of 1:50.8. His best for the mile came down to 4:04.4 before he took on the experienced Merv Lincoln, a man coached by Franz Stampfl, in the national championships. Lincoln led the way, but couldn't hold off the young Elliott who took over before the bell and won in 4:00.4.

After a southern hemisphere's winter of hard training, Elliott was soon to make his mark on the world. In January 1958 he became the youngest man to beat four minutes for the mile with a 3:59.9, and his domestic rivalry with Lincoln continued, with Elliott twice beating Stampfl's runner, the second time seeing them both awarded times of 3:59.6. He became national champion for both 880 yards and the mile, and after some races in the US was in the UK for the Empire Games. He was surprisingly beaten in a warm-up 880, but then was back on form to win both his events at Cardiff in July.

But then, on August 6, came one of the great races, and one of the truly outstanding world records.

Ireland was going athletics mad thanks to the success of Ron Delany at the Olympics of 1956, and Santry Stadium was built in Dublin. This was a cinder track remember, but it was hard and true – Australian

ABOVE & BELOW: Peter Snell took his talent around the world and was never afraid to take on the best, whether it be (above) in the United States – such as as the Compton Invitational in California in 1963 – or (below) in London against the best of Europe.

"Ibbotson was popular with the fans and press and ran a lot of races – often approaching 70 per season."

Albie Thomas had recently broken the three mile world record there – and the men about to compete were on good form. As well as Thomas, the in-form Delany and Elliott, the organisers had persuaded Lincoln and New Zealand track legend Murray Halberg, who would go on to win gold in the 5000 metres at the Rome Olympics and had taken part in the Bannister versus Landy clash in 1954, to also take part.

In front of a packed crowd Thomas took them through the first lap in 56 seconds, and although the pace slowed the half mile was hit in 1:58... and with plenty of top-class runners in contention. Elliott took over on the third lap and that should have been it... but no one had shown Merv Lincoln the script and the Aussie overtook his compatriot before the bell for the final lap. As Elliott said in his book The Golden Mile: "I had never known him to do such a thing at this stage of a race before. I was thunderstruck."

They hit the bell in 2:59 and then Elliott attacked again, overtaking Lincoln and trying to 'break' his old rival, but Stampfl's runner would not quit and was still with Elliott as they reached the final corner. On the home straight Elliott finally broke clear, and reached the line in 3:54.5, almost three seconds clear of Ibbotson's world record. Forgotten in the excitement of Elliott's world best was the fact that Lincoln had also beaten 'Ibbo's previous mark by finishing in 3:55.9, while Delany and Halberg tied at 3:57.5 and 'pacemaker' Thomas also dipped more than a second under the four minutes.

It was a memorable race, five men under four minutes for the first time in a single race, and a stunning world best mark... and as far as this publication is concerned we could leave Elliott's story there. But one of the all-time greats does deserve to have the rest of his brief running career acknowledged.

Elliott was academically brilliant and athletics was never going to be a long-term deal for him, however, a final target remained – the Rome Olympics of 1960. His 1959 was quiet after the massive efforts of the previous year which had taken in the Australian summer and then the European season too, but he built up steadily for Rome through 1960, and knew he was in good shape by running some personal bests at Cerutty's Portsea training base.

Of course this was the Olympics so it was the 1500 metres rather than the mile, an event at which Elliott already held the world record of 3:36.0. After a solid heat which he won, Elliott was confident going into the final and in that race made his move just after the halfway mark, and took the lead before the bell. Coach Percy Cerutty had told him he would wave a towel if Elliott was on world record pace, the towel was duly waved and the Australian ran as hard as he could for the final 200 ➤

BELOW: The next generation was coming through by the mid 1960s, with student Jim Ryun, the latest in a line of great Kansas athletes, beating Peter Snell (left) in San Diego on June 27, 1965.

metres, finishing a record 20 metres ahead of silver medal winner Michel Jazy. As statisticians like to point out, his winning time would also have won the gold medal in Seoul (1988), Barcelona (1992) and Atlanta (1996).

Elliott's top-class running career was nearly at an end, he was due to start at Cambridge that October and after that ran only intermittently. At senior level he remained unbeaten over 1500 metres or the mile... but that proud record was nearly lost towards the end of his career during early 1961. A young undergraduate called Martin Heath led the Olympic champion during a race, only to be beaten after a despairing effort in the final 15 yards. In January 1962, Elliott won a cross-country race for Cambridge against the Royal Navy, and just a week later his world mile record was beaten... the record journey was back on its downward path, and another man from Down Under had lowered the mark, just. The new name in the record book was the New Zealander Peter Snell.

One of the great things about sport is that athletes and performers from different eras don't meet while each is at their peak. Why is this great? Because it allows armchair experts and bar room pundits to pontificate over who was superior and why. Whether it's Ali versus Tyson or Marciano or Louis in the heavyweight boxing world, or Barcelona 2011 versus Brazil 1970, Ajax 1972 or Liverpool 1978 in football, no one really knows for sure. Similarly, two of the best middle distance runners didn't meet at their peaks even though they were separated by just a few years, and there are many who would place Sir Peter George Snell at the very top of the tree.

It's also perhaps remarkable that the New Zealander, who was born in 1938 and who won an Olympic 1500 metres (in Tokyo 1964) and lowered the mile record twice, is still seen by many mainly as an 800 metre runner.

A good all-round sportsman in his youth, it wasn't until he was 19 that he turned his attention to running and started work with coach Arthur Lydiard.

The coach's approach was that Snell, a big man and with a powerful physique, had good basic speed but needed endurance... given that, he could become a champion. So Lydiard had him training like a marathon runner, trying to build up to 100 miles a week. This endurance is what won him his 800 metres Olympic gold in Rome. This virtual unknown outside New Zealand was in an event for

ABOVE: Kenya's Kip Keino defeated Ryun at altitude in the 1968 Mexico Olympics by running a new Olympic record.

BELOW LEFT: Ryun went on to enjoy a career in politics, here sharing a stage with US President George W Bush, a fellow Republican.

which the organisers had scheduled two heats on the first day and then the semi-finals and final on the next two days. Coach Lydiard thought four races in three days would be perfect for Snell, and in his morning heat the Kiwi ran a personal best to win in 1:48.1.

In the afternoon he was close behind the Belgian Roger Moens in 1:48.6. The next day he won his semi-final in 1:47.2, another personal best, then it was time for the final. After going out hard, Snell found himself behind several runners with 200 to go and thought he had no chance. But in the last straight he remained on the inside, a gap opened and as others floundered, he came through to pip Moens. His strength had won him the title... now it was to pay dividends at the longer distance too.

After injury early in 1961, he returned to form with some fine wins later that season, but 1962 is when he enters the mile record books. His season started well with an 880 yard national record of 1:48, then lowered that to 1:47. At the end of January he was entered into the mile race at Cooks Gardens in Wanganui, and with marathons and 800s in his locker, he was clearly in record-breaking shape: "I knew my form was improving and that I was virtually certain to run under four minutes for the first time in my life," he said in the book No Bugles, No Drums which he wrote with Garth Gilmour.

It was a decent pace but nothing to write home about for the first two laps, reaching the half mile in 2:00.0. At the bell Bruce Tulloh went past him, but Snell stayed with the Englishman (who would win 5000 metres European gold later that year) and at the final bend Snell went for it. As he described it in his book: "I don't think I have ever felt such a glorious feeling of strength and speed."

He crossed the line in 3:54.4, a new world record by the most slender of margins... but a record all the same.

Snell went on a world record blitz, setting a remarkable 'double' of new marks for both the 800 metres and 880 yards, and despite an injury setback took double gold at the Empire and Commonwealth Games in Perth later in 1962. The following year he confirmed his mastery over both 800 and 1500, but entered Olympic year with some doubting his ability to bring back more gold after a mediocre start to the year. However, pre-Tokyo training went well, and despite going down with the flu just before the games, he recovered in time to do something which would prove beyond the abilities of men such as Coe, Ovett, Walker and El Guerrouj and complete the 800/1500 double, and he did it in style.

Later that year, and with the southern hemisphere season just starting, Snell was racing again, and this time lowered the world mile best at a meeting in Auckland, taking it down to 3:54.1.

CARR DRIVES THE MILE FORWARD

A number of annual mile races are held around the world and one of the most famous is the Emsley Carr Mile, first run in 1953 and inaugurated by Sir William Carr in memory of his father, Sir Emsley, a former editor of the *News of the World* newspaper.

The invitational race was introduced to encourage the achievement of the first sub-four minute mile, but by the time of the second event, Roger Bannister had already taken that record.

However, the race continued and is one of those prestigious events a top quality athlete likes to have on his CV.

The trophy comprises a book, bound in red Morocco leather, containing a history of mile running throughout the world since 1868 and signatures of many of the world's leading milers, including Paavo Nurmi, Sydney Wooderson, John Landy and Bannister, as well as all the winners.

The race has been won by 10 Olympic champions, including Hicham El Guerrouj, Kip Keino and John Walker, as well as British greats Steve Ovett and Sebastian Coe, while seven world mile record holders have taken the honours – Walker, Coe, Ovett, El Guerrouj, Jim Ryun, Derek Ibbotson and Filbert Bayi.

The winning time by current mile world record holder El Guerrouj in 2000 is the fastest so far at 3:45.96 – the fastest time ever in Britain – while the first man to win the event in under four minutes was Ibbotson, when he was victorious in 1956.

At the time this publication goes to press, the champion is Kenyan Augustine Choge (below), who won the 2013 event as part of the Anniversary Games in London's Olympic Stadium. Choge, who also won in 2010, is the former Commonwealth 5000 metres champion and ran 3:50.01 to edge out Djibouti's Ayanleh Souleiman.

The following year his form dipped... and he decided the time was right to retire and move on to other challenges. Interviewed by the Wanganui Chronicle in 2009 after a statue of him was unveiled, Snell admitted he had "never reached his potential" over the mile.

Barely seven months after Snell's second mile record, the second Frenchman to lower the mile record joined that elite list of athletes, yet Michel Jazy still rated Herb Elliott as "better than me, better than anyone".

Perhaps better at the longer distances of two miles and 5000 metres, where he also set world records, Jazy was still an excellent 1500 metres runner, having finished runner-up to Elliott in the 1960 Olympic final, and his sprint finish was enough to see off all but the very best.

The 20-year-old Jazy was part of the French team at the 1956 Melbourne Olympics and credits marathon runner Alain Mimoun as being a massive influence on him, for demonstrating the sacrifices needed to be one of the best. Apprenticed as a printer, after his national military service ended the French sports newspaper L'Equipe employed him, with the aim of helping him reach the top.

Jazy was a free spirit, and interval training and heavy track work was never for him, with the forest tracks and methods of Gosta Olander at Valadalen, Sweden far more to his liking. It had worked for Gunder Haegg and Jazy was next.

By the time of the Rome Olympics he was ready and although it was generally thought he could make the final, there was no real weight of expectation. Jazy enjoyed a clear run, avoiding getting boxed in, and when Elliott made his break with a lap to go the Frenchman responded. The Australian's lead was too much to haul back, but with a finishing time of 3:38.4 Jazy had arrived as a major player on the world stage.

Over the next few years European titles and medals followed, and for the 1964 Olympics he targeted the 5000 as the schedule made a 1500/5000 double ➤

virtually impossible, but one of those great 'what ifs' will also remain matching his sprint finish against Snell's in that 1964 1500 final...

Jazy was a star of the mid-Sixties, but never THE star in an era which was dominated by Elliott, Snell and then the next great thing... a teenage American prodigy. But he was a quality athlete and a man to be respected.

On June 30, 1965, he beat a superb field in a 5000 metres race in Helsinki to set a European record, and this came just three weeks after he lowered the mile record to 3:53.6 in a race at Rennes, a time which remained the European record until Eamonn Coghlan beat it a full decade later.

Irishman Coghlan, a keen student of athletics, has massive respect for Jazy and his achievements.

"There's a real fondness for that era, and those guys were top quality," he said. "Jazy will certainly go down in history and deserves to be mentioned in the same sentence at his contemporaries."

A relative veteran when at his peak, Jazy set nine world records between 1961 and 1966 – over the mile (once), 2000 metres (twice, 3000 metres (twice), the two miles (twice) and the 4 × 1500 metres relay (twice). Four of those were set in June 1965.

However, as hinted at, the next great thing wasn't just on the horizon, he was running rapidly to front and centre stage, and was another of those stars whose career was short but brilliant, and whose achievements bring us from the cinder track and national service era of Ibbotson to the bright lights and colour TV of the 1970s.

Jim Ryun has excelled on many fronts. To a younger generation of Americans he is the former Republican member of the House of Representatives, to an older generation he is one of athletics' record breakers who, for various reasons, was never able to fulfill his massive potential on the Olympic stage.

Born in 1947, here was another US runner from the state of Kansas about to make his mark. A gangly sports-mad kid who suffered from allergies, at his high school he was inspired by coach Bob Timmons to try our for athletics and after a stuttering start he became his school's top cross-country runner by the age of 15.

Ryun clocked some good times for the mile... and then got better, and better. Just days before his 16th birthday he recorded 4:19.7, then lowered that to 4:07.8 just months later.

Timmons' approach was for a massive workload and at 16 Ryun was training twice a day and running more than 100 miles a week, with some famously intense sessions as part of that.

The times he was recording meant he was included in races against some of the US's top men and he proved competitive, in one early race finishing third in 4:01.7. His next event was against a strong field which included 1960 Olympian Jim Grelle, and although Ryun finished eighth he was timed at 3:59.0... and became the first schoolboy to break four minutes, a mere decade after Bannister's feats at Oxford.

He managed to qualify for the Olympics as a 17-year-old and didn't disgrace himself, going out in the semi-final which featured Snell.

ABOVE: Michel Jazy was Europe's great hope in an era dominated by men such as Elliott, Snell and the young Jim Ryun.

BELOW & ABOVE RIGHT: Ryun is another world great who has his name on the list of Emsley Carr Mile winners, here taking the tape in 1967.

The following season, with a new coach as Timmons had moved on to the University of Kansas, Ryun came through after a slight injury setback. In a race at Modesto he was up against Olympic silver medalist Josef Odlozil of Czechoslovakia. He took the bell in 3:01.9 but saw Grelle overtake him… however, Ryun was not finished and edged past to win in 3:58.1. An impressive personal best.

A great season's racing followed, including some against Snell – a man Ryun admitted he feared the first time they raced, but then realised he could compete. At San Diego it was another battle with Grelle with Snell charging for the line, but Ryun held the Olympic legend off with a final lap of 53.9 to win in 3:55.3.

Ryun started at the University of Kansas and was reunited with Timmons, and expectation was growing for the 1966 season. Although Jazy's mile mark was clearly a target, the first world best he took was Snell's 880 yard best, lowering it 1:45.1 to 1:44.9, then in Berkeley it was time for a go at Jazy's record. After an opening lap of 57.9 and reaching halfway in 1:55.5, Ryun went on his own in lap three as the pace slowed. He needed 58.3 to break the record… and did it in 56.0 for a staggering new world record of 3:51.3.

"I didn't know it was a world record until they announced it over the loudspeaker. I was surprised," Ryun said.

The following year, after recovering from an injury which curtailed his cross country season, and with the Olympics on the horizon, Ryun was again in record-breaking form. The next major 'barrier' for the mile was 3:50… and Ryun was clearly favourite to do this.

In June, and after a week's altitude training, he set out to break 3:50 in the AAU Championships. He led from the start but after laps of 59, 60 and then 58.5 he seemed well off the pace for a record. However, a burst of pace saw a staggering last lap of 53.7… and another new world record. He hadn't cracked 3:50, but 3:51.1 had taken the record even further away. Soon after, in a race with Kip Keino, he broke the 1500 metres record too.

He needed 58.3 to break the record… and did it in 56.0.

"I didn't know it was a record until they announced it over the loudspeaker."

As far as the mile record is concerned, Ryun had taken it to a place where no one could reach for nearly a decade, however, his athletics story continued, and although some may see parts as a disappointment, that would be harsh.

In 1968 the Olympics were in Mexico and at altitude, and placing his great rival, the Kenyan Kip Keino, at an advantage. Both men had problems oing into the games with their fitness, but Keino was simply too strong for any runner not used to such conditions, and Ryun's silver medal was a great achievement.

The weight of expectation and pressure was proving too much for Ryun, by now newly married. "I'd burned myself out; the competitive edge was gone," he later said.

After a long break, his wife Anne persuaded him to start running again, and he even entertained thoughts of the 1972 Olympics in Munich, so hard training followed, and he made the plane after running himself into form.

And it a strange way it was perhaps the mile which did for his Olympic hopes in 1972. In one of his races which proved he was getting back to form he had recorded a mile time of 3:52. In Munich, and for the seeding process, someone had this as a time for the shorter 1500 metres, so he was placed in the wrong heat. During that preliminary round race, and while battling for position with just over a lap to go, he was spiked in his foot and fell with a runner from Ghana, whose knee struck him in the head.

Ryun eventually climbed back to his feet with the rest of the runners out of sight. He still finished in 3:51.52, but despite two appeals his Olympic dream was over at last.

His later career was spent running professionally, organising running camps, getting involved with his church and national politics. But his mile record would take us into a new decade… and the first African to enter the list. ∎

ABOVE: Greats shake – Kenya's Kip Keino shares a smile with rival Jim Ryun in 1965.

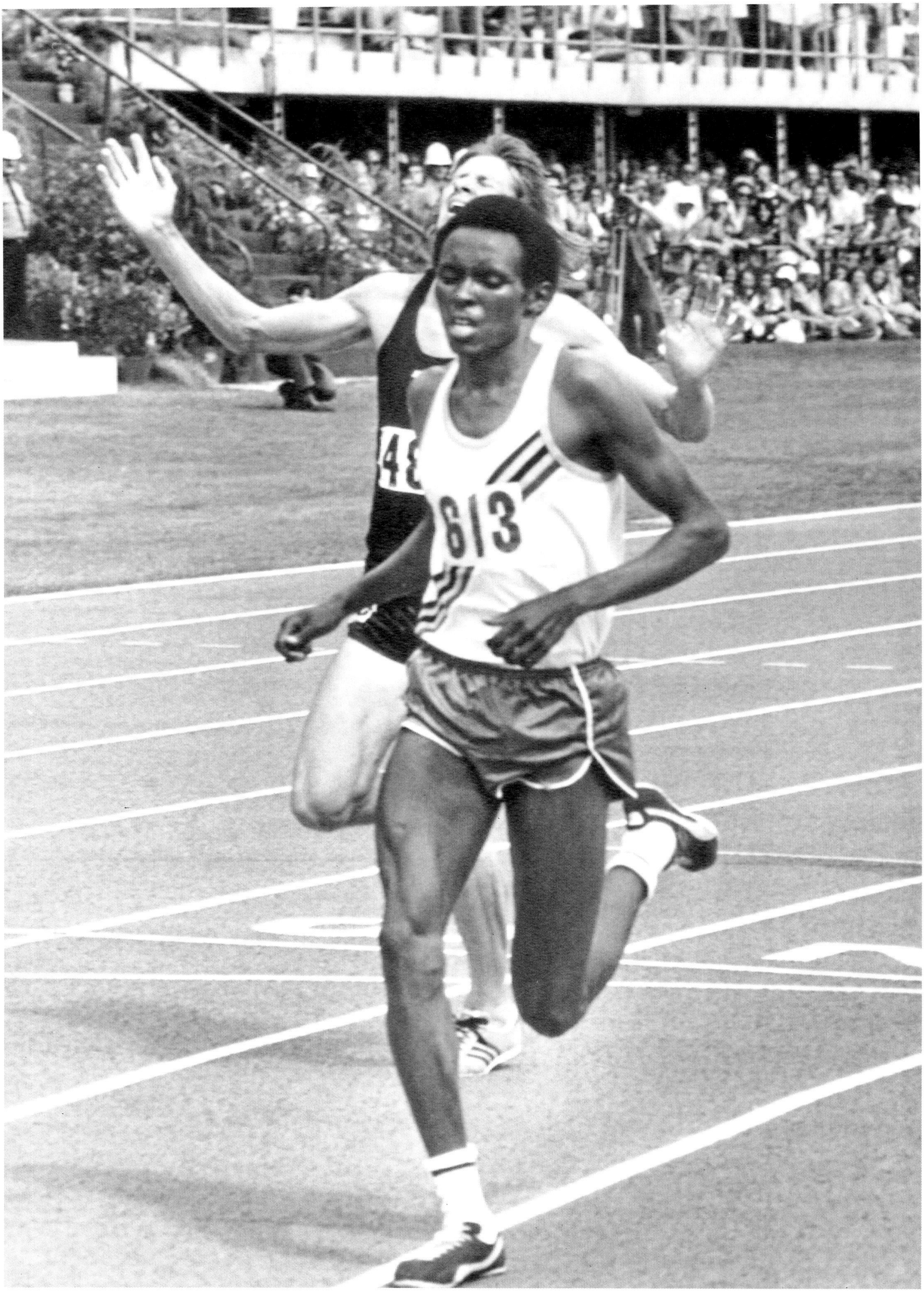

613

African first, runner Walker...
and the
best of British

The quality of Jim Ryun's world records for the mile and 1500 metres may be difficult to comprehend all these years later, and for a publication which is concentrating on the mile, readers will hopefully forgive a brief discussion about the metric distance because, as we've already seen, these distances are linked throughout the Olympic era.

What is clear is that it took a special run, and one which changed the way the middle distances could be approached, to finally beat Ryun's seven-year-old 1500 world best at the 1974 Commonwealth Games in Christchurch, New Zealand, and set the scene for the American's mile best to be beaten the following year by the same two men who would dominate this metric mile version for the next part of our tale.

Britons with a rose-tinted view may think of this early Seventies period as simply marking time before Ovett and Coe, but that would be wrong, and wouldn't do justice to two greats of athletics who each made a real mark on the sport; Filbert Bayi – the first African to hold the world mile record, and John Walker, a man who would enjoy a remarkable period at the very top and feature in so many of the middle distance great encounters of the next decade or more.

As it is we have already skipped past a number of excellent athletes... but needs must when the story flies by at breakneck pace... and the fact years pass before the record comes under threat is proof if ever it were needed of Ryun's quality.

New Zealand has already featured heavily in this story through the likes of Lovelock and Snell, and certainly does for the next few significant years and events, as politics and sport were mixed like a cheap cocktail to impact upon the Olympics for years to come – whether it was the terrorist attack at Munich in 1972, the African nations' boycott of Montreal 1976 following ➤

FAR LEFT: Filbert Bayi shatters the world 1500 metres record in 1974.

ABOVE: After missing the 1976 Olympics, Bayi was still a force for the rest of the decade, here winning the Golden Mile at Crystal Palace in 1980... with a young Steve Cram in the distance.

LEFT: Bayi enjoyed the Moscow sights... and took steeplechase silver.

FOUR MINUTE MILE 93

RIGHT: New Zealand's John Walker (694) heads a young Steve Ovett (375) in the semi-final of the Olympic 1500 metres in Montreal.

BELOW: Ireland's Eamonn Coghlan and John Walker lead the pack in the 1500 metres final in Montreal, ahead of Britain's Frank Clement, Belgian Ivo van Damme and West Germany's Paul-Heinz Wellmann.

the All Blacks rugby tour of apartheid South Africa, the United States' withdrawal from Moscow in 1980 in protest at the Soviet Union's 'intervention' in Afghanistan, or the tit-for-tat boycott by the Eastern Bloc of 1984's Los Angeles games on a flimsy 'safety' excuse.

But for this part of our story, New Zealand in 1974 was the warm and friendly venue for a world record worthy of a host of superlatives, and one which brought a brilliant rivalry to the attention of the sporting world.

Forty years on (at the time of writing, Glasgow 2014 is still to happen) diminutive Tanzanian Filbert Bayi's 3:32.16 is still the Commonwealth record for 1500 metres. But it wasn't just the time which caused those in the know to sit up and take note, it was his style, as well as that of the hard-charging home favourite who nearly beat him.

As the BBC commentator David Coleman memorably reported at the time, the "tiny Tanzanian" had led "from gun to tape". This is another event it's well worth searching for on video sharing websites, as Coleman's apt phrasing adds atmosphere to an already special race. His description of home favourites Rod Dixon and John Walker as the "black shadows" looming over Bayi adds to the drama... as does the stark reality when he announces that Jim Ryun's world record had "been taken apart".

Bayi's superb effort in New Zealand was not carefully planned with pacemakers, instead it was him, taking the challenge to the others and seeing who could stand up to him.

Walker went under Ryun's old world record of 3:33.1, while third place Ben Jipcho of Kenya, fourth placed Dixon and fifth placed Graham Crouch ran the fourth, fifth and seventh fastest times at that point. There was no jostling for position, the usual battles and psychology in a major championship 1500 metres, instead Bayi went to the front... and stayed there. He was a staggering 20 metres ahead at 800 metres with the others in a long line, and when spectators thought the Tanzanian would fade, he simply kept going to the line.

Decades later Bayi would say: "Think about the change that occurred in the 1500 metres at Christchurch. The 1500 metres was usually a slow race and then a sprint. But in 1974 I changed that from the beginning to the end. And not many people have thought about that."

One who has is Sebastian Coe, as although people such as David Moorcroft – a top-class miler and former world 5000 metre record holder – credit Coe (and Steve Ovett) with pushing a host of athletes to great times by being fast 'from the off', Coe himself knows where his inspiration came from.

"I changed the face of 800 metres running. I don't think I changed the face of 1500 metres running. Bayi did that." It was Coe who would eventually take that 1500 metres record five years later in Zurich.

Bayi realises he is often a 'forgotten man' – he has never been inducted into the IAAF hall of fame. "My Commonwealth Games record has stood for 40 years but people never talk about Filbert Bayi," he says.

"I can say 100% that I did not get the credit I deserved for it. Maybe when I die they will say he was the one who broke the record that lived as long as he did. I have attended the games so many times but never have they announced they have the 1500 metre record holder sitting in the stadium. It would be nice to feel it has been recognised."

"Maybe when I die they will say he was the one who broke the record that lived as long as he did. It would be nice to feel it has been recognised."

Bayi's 1500 metres in New Zealand was one of the great records and lasted until 1979, surviving through one of the most competitive eras in these distances. But as far as this publication is concerned, it was the following year, and another record, which comes under scrutiny, and this time it took an equally great race to relieve Ryun of another of his records. However, this time the new record would last barely three months.

The setting for the first episode in the lowering of the mile best – the first time it was to happen in the 1970s – was Kingston, Jamaica.

The event had attracted some of the sport's biggest names, including some rising talent who would do battle on the tracks of the world for years to come.

Filbert Bayi, still just 21 years old, was already in good form, having won impressively in Italy over 1000 metres (2:18.1) and 800 metres (1:48.3) and was up against two men from Villanova University in Pennsylvania, US, a hot bed of track and field under renowned coach 'Jumbo' Elliott.

Marty Liquori, 25, had been on the scene for a few years, beating Jim Ryun in 1971 and boasted a best time of 3:53.6, while Irish 21-year-old Eamonn Coghlan was just starting to make a name for himself and had run 3:56.2 just a fortnight earlier.

Also in the field was American Rick Wohlhuter, the fastest man over 800 metres in 1974 (1:43.4), and a promising 1500 runner with 3:39.7 to his credit (he would go on to finish sixth in the 1500 at Montreal and take bronze in the 800 behind the Cuban star Alberto Juantorena), plus world indoor mile record holder Tony Waldrop. His indoor mark of 3:55.0 set in 1974 had eclipsed another Ryun record and he also had an outdoor best of 3:53.2.

The crowd were right behind Bayi despite the presence of their own Sylvan Barrett, and it was the Tanzanian who took the lead early, stretching several yards ahead of Britain's Walter Wilkinson and Coghlan.

Bayi went through the first lap in 56.9 and was a dozen yards up on the young Irishman, then proceeded to stretch his lead further still on lap two, at which point Coghlan responded, followed by Liquori. At the halfway mark Coghlan (1:58.0) and Liquori (1:58.4) were still 10 yards down and chasing hard, and the massive effort continued on lap three as approaching the bell Coghlan was on Bayi's shoulder and Liquori had almost joined them.

The African took the bell in 2:55.3 with Coghlan four tenths down and Liquori hanging on, but Bayi was winding up the pressure, varying the pace, almost toying with his opponents, and as they reached the final bend Liquori finally passed the tiring Irishman and attempted to close the four yard gap to Bayi. Instead the margin widened... and continued to grow so that by the end he was 1.2 seconds clear, and more importantly stopped the clock at 3:51.0, just 0.1 inside Ryun's old world best.

Experts point to Bayi's tactics as being remarkable for what was a world record run, as his pace varied throughout, hardly seeming conducive to setting such a time, as was his style of running relatively wide.

What the race did was bring Liquori and Coghlan to the attention of the wider athletics public, especially the Irishman who set a new personal best of 3:53.3 in Jamaica, just a week after his previous record of 3:56.2. The times were a massive breakthrough, as he said earlier this year: "When I did run sub-four, it was like 'holy sh*t! I went 3.56, then very quickly a 3.53... and I was being talked about. But even so, for me the focus was Montreal and the Olympics the year after." ➤

ABOVE: Walker and van Damme on the Montreal podium.

FOUR MINUTE MILE 95

What Coghlan had done was break the European record of Jazy which had stood for a decade and had been the world best until Ryun destroyed it.

Coghlan would have many battles with the next man to hold the mile record, an athlete who grew up in rural New Zealand and who, as a child 'ran everywhere'.

John Walker, perhaps second only to Roger Bannister, is often the man next 'most associated' with the sub-four minute mile… for the sheer number he racked up during an impressive career.

His first was in Victoria, British Columbia's Centennial Stadium on July 7, 1973, during a five nations meet between hosts Canada, Australia, New Zealand, Japan and the US, and he went on to run 135 sub-four miles… and if the 1500 metres wasn't the 'distance of choice' at major championships, the chances are he'd have gone on to run more than 200.

Throughout his career at the top Walker was coached by Arch Jelley, a school principal, and a middle distance runner himself, and the coach had a meticulous approach.

Walker said: "I followed his schedules exactly. We kept in close contact and Arch used to write very long letters. We spent a 20 year period as athlete and coach and we worked well together. When he set schedules, I set out to better them. I always tried to impress him. I trained really hard." But even though he trained hard, he admits he hated it and instead simply loved racing.

"I ran 80 miles per week when not racing and 60 miles per week in race season. I was fit all year round – indoors, New Zealand season and European season. I hated training but this was the secret of my success."

One of the New Zealander's career highlights came in the (northern hemisphere) summer of 1975, when the 23-year-old lowered the record to exactly 10 seconds faster than Bannister had run at Oxford on that May evening.

In 77 degree heat on August 12, Walker made sure the event in Gothenburg would enter the history books after running what he called "a perfect race".

Straight after the event he told the world's press: "I didn't believe I had a chance. I've been thinking it over and over the last few days – how to run, how to beat it (the record). Now I feel I couldn't have run a more perfect race."

Sweden's Goran Savemark was key to the record, as he set a good pace for the New Zealander, who was timed at 56.3 seconds for the first lap, went through 880 yards in 1:55.5 and took the lead on the third lap, outstripping Australians Ken Hall and Graeme Crouch as he pushed on and took the bell at 2:53.5.

For the last lap Walker eclipsed Bayi's short-lived world best when he ran the last lap in less than 56 seconds, to finish in 3:49.4.

The front-running African's record had gone, and for Walker it was a significant mark, and one he was desperate to follow-up by beating his rival after suffering three reverses during 1975, the usual pattern being that Bayi's pace at the front had proven a fraction too much for the quick finishing Kiwi.

It seemed there would be years of the Walker versus Bayi rivalry, yet events took over and other athletes emerged, making that 1974 Commonwealth clash the greatest encounter between the pair.

As mentioned, the African nations' boycott of the Montreal Olympics meant they were not to meet on the biggest stage, but even then chances are it wouldn't have happened as Bayi fell ill with malaria shortly before the Olympics.

Walker went into the games as favourite and after he and coach Jelley focused on how to beat Bayi, plans had to quickly change as in the final he instead faced a field full of fast finishers rather than the front runner. As the

ABOVE & LEFT: Irishman Eamonn Coghlan was one of the top runners through the 1970s and 80s, along with American Steve Scott (in second place in the picture above). Scott holds the record for sub-four miles – having run 136, while Coghlan ran a sub-four when aged over 40, and held the indoor record for more than a decade.

RIGHT: Coghlan was there to congratulate Bernard Lagat when he broke his record of wins in the Wanamaker Mile (see panel, opposite page).

race went on the New Zealander was worried that it was still too slow and he was in danger of losing to the 'kickers'... but then Coghlan perhaps lost his own chance of gold by going too soon. With just under 300 metres to go the Irishman took the pace on, and Walker followed... before surging into the lead.

Walker held on to win gold in a time of 3:39.17, with Belgian Ivo van Damme second and Paul-Heinz Wellmann of West Germany in third, Coghlan eventually coming fourth – the iconic image of the man in the black vest, arms outstretched as he crossed the line, became one of the pictures of that games.

Bayi's presence was missed, and it's one of the great 'what ifs' of sport as to how he would have fared that summer... if he had been fit.

The Tanzanian went on to win silver in the 3000 metres steeplechase at the 1980 Olympics in Moscow – running 8:12.5 behind Poland's Bronisław Malinowski, a man who would be killed in a car crash the following year, while he also defended his All-Africa 1500 metres title in 1978. After retiring he set up the Filbert Bayi Foundation which aims to guide sporting talent in Tanzania.

Walker would remain a force in middle distance running for many years to come, but although he was often at the top table, his exploits became much more ➤

ALL A BOARD...
THE INDOOR STORY

When it comes to excitement and atmosphere, it's often very difficult to beat something the North Americans seem to have mastered staging, and the Irish have time and again proved winners at.

Run indoors, the mile has a certain magic, including a shorter track – usually 200 metres, usually banked, and often wooden boards. Add in the contained noise an arena with a roof provides, and you have a brilliant amphitheatre. And although the world record times have always lagged slightly behind their outdoor equivalents – shorter straights will always mean less chance to build that extra leg speed – there are still great times.

One of the most famous races in the world is the Wanamaker Mile, held as part of the Millrose Games every February in New York.

It was actually first held in 1908, but in 1926 the race became known as the Wanamaker in honour of the head of the eponymous department store, Rodman Wanamaker.

The names on the roll call of winners include many of the greats of mile running – indoors or out, but one nation which has always embraced the event (apart from the US) is Ireland, and winners have included Ron Delany, Marcus O'Sullivan and the man dubbed the 'chairman of the boards' – Eamonn Coghlan. His record of seven wins was finally surpassed by Kenya-born American Bernard Lagat in 2010, and Coghlan was there to greet him when he took his record.

"I was brought up as a racer, and I had a real love affair with running indoors. I seemed to be able to run faster around those tight bends, and the more I did it, the better I felt," Coghlan told the author. "I loved the rhythm, the beat of the boards, the rush it gave me... and it got so that I didn't get the same feeling outdoors - even though I still enjoyed success outdoors, especially when I moved up to 5000 metres."

The current world record holder is, surprise surprise, Hicham El Guerrouj... his February 1997 time of 3:48.45 finally knocking Coghlan off the top of the pile after his 18 years as number one. And that list of world record holders includes such quality runners as Gunnar Nielsen, Wes Santee, Gil Dodds, Glenn Cunningham and Paavo Nurmi. The current Wanamaker holder is Will Leer (pictured below).

FOUR MINUTE MILE 97

about his tally of sub-four runs as in 1985 he became the first man to run 100 such times, just beating the American Steve Scott to the mark.

Now in his early sixties, Sir John Walker is a councillor and businessman in Auckland – in 1996, just a couple of years after retiring from the track, it was announced this athletics great was suffering from Parkinson's disease.

The man who would break both Bayi's 1500 metre best, and Walker's mile mark, would take those records during a remarkable athletic summer of 1979, and he continues to play a massive part in sport in the UK more than three decades on.

Sebastian Newbold (Seb) Coe was the first mile record holder to be born after Sir Roger Bannister's feats at Oxford six decades ago, and the Briton's career is inextricably linked to that of his great British rival – Stephen Michael James (Steve) Ovett.

It's easy to become self-absorbed, to think that your sports teams or athletes are 'world class' when they perhaps aren't, to assume the rest of the globe is as interested in your own domestic affairs as you are. But in the late 1970s and early 1980s it really was true that Great Britain had a production line of men's talent in the middle distances.

At the 1976 Olympic Games in Montreal it was an oft-overlooked Scot who flew the flag for Britain in the men's 1500 metres, Frank Clement battling to fifth place in the final in Canada. The Bellahouston Harrier was a quality runner who was always 'there or thereabouts', winning the European Cup final in 1973, as well as the World Student Games and Emsley Carr

Mile that same year. But the day after John Walker won gold, perhaps very few British athletics fans would have laid money on the fact that by the next Olympics the 1500 metres and 800 metres (and indeed the mile, which for a short period in this story takes second place) would be a cause of national obsession, pride and rivalry.

Casual sports fans, those whose expertise was gained from the armchair and tabloid back pages, could name a handful of British athletes during this period, from Geoff Capes to Brendan Foster, yet when it came to the middle distances the public seemed to be required to make a choice... were you in the Sebastian Coe camp, or a supporter of Steve Ovett? One the 'posh' boy who was eloquent and media savvy, the other a working class hero, loner and outsider who didn't talk to the press. Or at least that was the image.

In July 1980 the rivalry seemed to reach fever pitch, with ITN's News at Ten providing 'computer analysis' of who would win the 800 metres and 1500 metres in Moscow... and getting it 100% wrong. Of course, that rivalry and drama, the beauty and unpredictability is what makes sport, and a film version of the rivalry has long been in the pipeline.

The 'Coe versus Ovett' scenario had been developing for years, made all the more intriguing by the fact that the two hadn't been racing against each other in any of the major events of the athletics circuit, and for two or three years they had been the dominant names in a host of distances.

London-born Coe was brought up in Sheffield and coached by his father Peter, a man with no background in the sport but who had a massive ambition and a huge influence on his son's career. Young 'Seb' became Yorkshire Colts cross country champion at age 14, while at 16 he was English Schools Intermediate 3000 metres winner. But that was a year after the first clash in the Ovett and Coe rivalry... and very ordinary it was too, as at 1972's English Schools Cross Country Championships a 15-year-old Coe finished 10th while Stephen Ovett, then 16, came second.

Coe was clearly a talent though, and progressed through the domestic ranks, and after finishing third in the European Junior 1500m in 1975, his first major title arrived in superb fashion two years later when he won the 800 metres at the European Indoor Championships in San Sebastian in 1:46.54, front running... and destroying a very good field.

Later that summer, just a month before his 21st birthday, he won the Emsley Carr Mile, out-sprinting Filbert Bayi to come home in 3:57.7, and less than a fortnight later took his first national outdoor record, running the 800 metres in 1:44.95.

Meanwhile, the Steve Ovett story was already advancing apace. A year older than Coe, Ovett joined Brighton & Hove Athletics club in 1969 and emerged ➤

> *"Now aged in his early sixties, Sir John Walker is a councillor and businessman. A couple of years after retiring it was announced he had Parkinson's."*

LEFT & ABOVE: The greatest of rivals, Sebastian Coe had to admit second best to Steve Ovett in 'his' event, the 800 metres at Moscow in 1980.

FOUR MINUTE MILE 99

as a talented 400 metres runner. After success at English Schools level, he won AAA Youth titles in 1971 and 1972, then stepped onto the international scene in 1973 when he won the 800 metres at the European Junior Championships in 1:47.53.

Blooded in a major championship at the European Championships in Rome the following summer, he recorded a European Junior 800 metres best of 1:45.77 in a race won by Yugoslavia's Luciano Sušanj in 1:44.07, and his experience continued to grow when he competed at the Montreal Olympics, reaching the 1500 metres semi-finals and finishing fifth in the 800 metres.

The following summer Ovett took centre stage, winning the 1500 metres at the inaugural IAAF World Cup in Dusseldorf in a UK record of 3:34.45, ahead of West German Thomas Wessinghage and East Germany's Jurgen Straub, while in 1978 he won the European 1500 metres in Prague in 3:35.59 ahead of that world class miler Eamonn Coghlan (3:36.57) and fellow Briton David Moorcroft (3:36.70).

But it was at that same championship when Ovett and Coe clashed again... and the victor was... totally unexpected.

RIGHT: Steve Ovett never enjoyed a great relationship with the British press, but occasionally they caught a smile on the face of the Olympic champion and world mile record holder.

BELOW: By the 1983 World Championships Steve Cram had matured into another British middle distance great.

Coe and Ovett had dominated the early rounds of the 800 metres, with the other qualifying races won by East Germans Olaf Beyer and Andreas Busse, and those four dominated the semi-finals too, the Britons being favourites by quite a margin as they went into the final.

In his fascinating book The Perfect Distance, a publication highly recommended for a much more fulsome description of the rivalry of these great Britons, author Pat Butcher describes how Seb Coe and his father Peter had a plan for the final, and it was to go out as quickly as possible, and hang on... and hang on. Butcher quotes Coe junior as saying his father told him: "I want to know at the end of this race what these b******s are made of. And it's probably not enough to win, but it will get you onto the rostrum."

And Coe set off at a fantastic pace, running the first 400 metres in 49.3 seconds, but he wasn't alone. Ovett was prowling and Butcher quotes the older man as saying: "I'd realised I was in terrific shape, and Seb went off very fast. I remember thinking, I don't feel tired. It was disconcerting. I was clicking my heels behind him, and I kept thinking down the back straight, when is he going to 'go'? It took me 200 metres before I realised he wasn't going to go; he was flat out.'

Ovett moved past Coe... but then out of nowhere a blue vest went flying past both.

The watching David Moorcroft said: "With 200 to go I was convinced Seb was going to win. With 100 to go, I was convinced Steve was going to win. With probably 50 to go, I was even more convinced Steve was going to win."

But Beyer was victorious, knocking two seconds off his previous best time to take gold in a time of 1:43.84. Ovett took silver in a new British record of 1:44.09, while Coe came in third in 1:44.76.

The press, who had been building the rivalry between the two, may have been hoping that Coe and Ovett exchanged terse words afterwards, but as Ovett told the *Daily Mirror's* Mike Walters years later: "Seb's version is that when I came over to him after the race, I supposedly asked him, 'Who the **** was that?' But the truth is a bit more prosaic. I made the fatal mistake of concentrating on one man instead of the race itself. Although I was feeling really good, I slowed down to stay on Seb's shoulder and I remember thinking, 'The little bugger is holding something back'. I waited to make my move, and by the time I went past him I realised he hadn't got anything left in his locker. But the trouble was Olaf, who came past me on the straight like the fast train to Berlin.

"Seb was on all fours afterwards, completely knackered, and I just asked if he was okay, and he asked me, 'Did you win?' When I replied, 'No, not me', I think he might have been pleased. When Seb retells the story now, he adds that after-dinner punchline for comic effect."

Ovett had done enough at that championships to endear him to the British public, or at least enough of those who voted in the BBC Sports Personality of the Year, as he won that title for 1978 ahead of decathlete Daley Thompson and cricketer Ian Botham.

The next season was a remarkable one, both in terms of records, but also in the growing publicity, rivalry and controversy involving both Coe and Ovett... and it's now that we start to include the mile again... but not before another quick trip to Scandinavia.

Both men had clashes with UK athletics chiefs over getting 'permission' to run on what was quickly becoming an athletics 'circuit', but Ovett was always portrayed as the more awkward, mainly because of his unwillingness to give interviews with all but a select few journalists. And it was following Coe's insistence on travelling to Oslo for a meeting on July 5 that saw him become the first of the two to take a world record. In the 800 metres he followed Jamaican Lennie Smith through the first lap in 50.6 seconds but unlike the previous year in Prague he kept his form to cross the line in 1:42.33 (officially recognised as 1:42.40), destroying what many thought was a brilliant Alberto Juantorena world record – set at Montreal in 1976 – by more than a second.

Clearly in fantastic form, the new 800 metres world record holder was included in the Dream Mile field in Oslo just 12 days later – Ovett wasn't running, he was the dominant figure over the distance at that time, but was quoted as saying since Britain was providing several of the top runners for the distance, the race should be on UK shores.

Even so, the field was of top quality, including John Walker, Eamonn Coghlan, three Americans including Steve Scott plus four Britons – Graham Williamson, ➤

ABOVE: Coe's turn... the 1500 metres in Moscow saw Coe beat East Germany's Jurgen Straub into silver and Ovett into bronze medal position.

FOUR MINUTE MILE 101

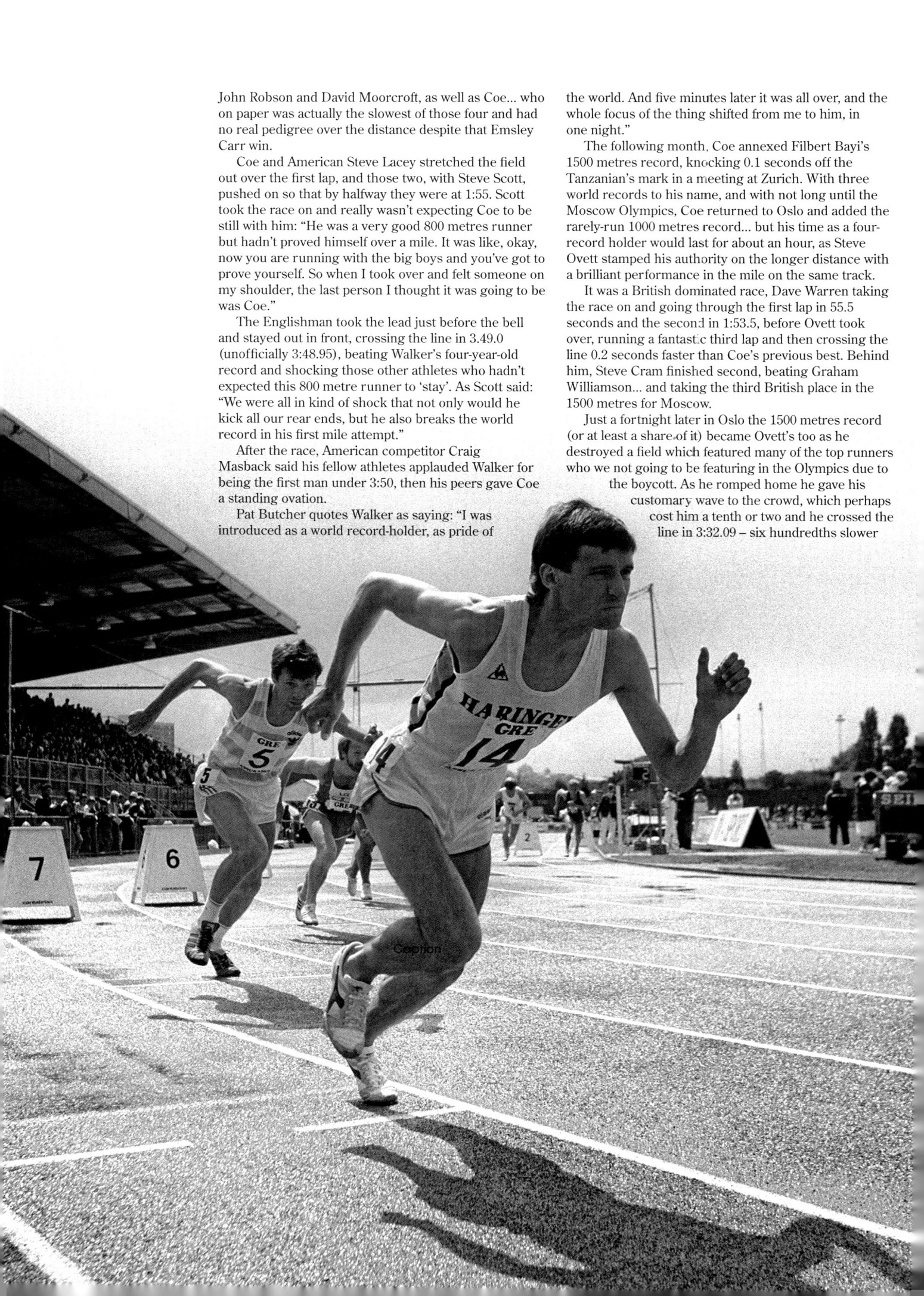

John Robson and David Moorcroft, as well as Coe... who on paper was actually the slowest of those four and had no real pedigree over the distance despite that Emsley Carr win.

Coe and American Steve Lacey stretched the field out over the first lap, and those two, with Steve Scott, pushed on so that by halfway they were at 1:55. Scott took the race on and really wasn't expecting Coe to be still with him: "He was a very good 800 metres runner but hadn't proved himself over a mile. It was like, okay, now you are running with the big boys and you've got to prove yourself. So when I took over and felt someone on my shoulder, the last person I thought it was going to be was Coe."

The Englishman took the lead just before the bell and stayed out in front, crossing the line in 3.49.0 (unofficially 3:48.95), beating Walker's four-year-old record and shocking those other athletes who hadn't expected this 800 metre runner to 'stay'. As Scott said: "We were all in kind of shock that not only would he kick all our rear ends, but he also breaks the world record in his first mile attempt."

After the race, American competitor Craig Masback said his fellow athletes applauded Walker for being the first man under 3:50, then his peers gave Coe a standing ovation.

Pat Butcher quotes Walker as saying: "I was introduced as a world record-holder, as pride of the world. And five minutes later it was all over, and the whole focus of the thing shifted from me to him, in one night."

The following month, Coe annexed Filbert Bayi's 1500 metres record, knocking 0.1 seconds off the Tanzanian's mark in a meeting at Zurich. With three world records to his name, and with not long until the Moscow Olympics, Coe returned to Oslo and added the rarely-run 1000 metres record... but his time as a four-record holder would last for about an hour, as Steve Ovett stamped his authority on the longer distance with a brilliant performance in the mile on the same track.

It was a British dominated race, Dave Warren taking the race on and going through the first lap in 55.5 seconds and the second in 1:53.5, before Ovett took over, running a fantastic third lap and then crossing the line 0.2 seconds faster than Coe's previous best. Behind him, Steve Cram finished second, beating Graham Williamson... and taking the third British place in the 1500 metres for Moscow.

Just a fortnight later in Oslo the 1500 metres record (or at least a share of it) became Ovett's too as he destroyed a field which featured many of the top runners who we not going to be featuring in the Olympics due to the boycott. As he romped home he gave his customary wave to the crowd, which perhaps cost him a tenth or two and he crossed the line in 3:32.09 – six hundredths slower

Caption

than Coe, but under the timing rules at the time it was 3:32.1 and a share of the world best.

It was the perfect build-up to the Moscow Olympics, to the clashes which would capture the imaginations of millions – neither of which were over the mile, but these two great milers dominated many of the games' headlines.

Far more has and will be written about these clashes, about the predictions, the press hype, the rivalry. For this publication it's simply a very interesting and poignant 'side tale' in the story of the mile and the milers, as the first event was the 800 metres, Coe's distance. But in the final he got his tactics wrong – whether it was pre-race nerves no one but Coe will ever know – and instead of a predicted fast early pace which would have suited the smaller Coe, it was a slow first lap. At one point Ovett was boxed in by the East German runners, but he manoeuvred the race brilliantly while Coe left himself far too much to do on the home straight. Master tactician Ovett won in 1:45.40 from Coe in 1:45.85 and Nikolay Kirov of the Soviet Union third.

For Coe it was a disaster, and what's more he wasn't favoured to bounce back in the second of the middle distances because Ovett was unbeaten in 45 races over a mile and 1500 metres. However, Coe gave one of the most stunning performances in Olympic history, while for Ovett the story was different – whether it was press attention at home on his girlfriend to whom it was assumed he'd waved 'ILY – I Love You' on the home straight in his races, or because he was complacent having now become an Olympic champion, or simply that Coe was determined and ran the better race.

This time Coe kept any nerves in check and flew down the home straight to win the 1500 metres in 3:38.40 with Ovett third in 3:38.99. They were separated by East German Jurgen Straub.

The story of each man would continue, taking in a variety of highs and lows both on and off the track. Coe would never reclaim the 1500 metres world record, which was lowered again by Ovett in Koblenz later that summer, by South African-born American Sydney Maree in August 1983, and then just a week after that by Ovett again in Rieti, Italy, before the 'youngster' of the ➤

TOP: Another world record Coe was part of was the 4 x 800 metres best of 7:03.89 alongside Peter Elliott, Steve Cram and Garry Cook.

ABOVE & LEFT: Sebastian Coe celebrates winning gold as he crosses the line ahead of Straub and Ovett in Moscow.

great British trio, Steve Cram, took it below 3:30. However, when we come to the mile, there was another golden summer – indeed, a golden nine days – to come in 1981, when both men were in peak form.

Coe lowered the 800 metres world best time to 1:41.73 in Florence in June 1981, before on July 11 he took his 1000 metre mark to 2:12.18 from 2:13.40.

Then on August 19, at the Letzigrund in Zurich, Coe broke the mile world record with 3:48.53 in Zurich, his third world record of the summer. Tom Byers had been enlisted as the pacemaker, but suffering from a cold he struggled to keep on schedule after a decent first lap, meaning Coe had to work very hard on his own over the final lap-and-a-half.

Ovett, who had been struggling with a leg injury, was motivated to regain his record, and just a week later, this time at the small stadium in Koblenz where he'd taken

ABOVE & BELOW: A year's difference in these two pictures, as in 1976 Sebastian Coe trails behind winner David Moorcroft as he wins the Emsley Carr Mile at Crystal Palace.
A year later, Coe breasted the tape ahead of former mile world record holder Filbert Bayi to take the Emsley Carr race.

the 1500 metres record the year before, he persuaded the organisers to add a mile to the schedule which already included a 1500 metres race.

Bob Benn took up the early pace before James Robinson took up the mantle on lap three, leaving Ovett just over a lap to go it alone. He did... scorching home on his own in 3:48.4.

Was that it? Of course not... now it was Coe's turn, and 48 hours later the Golden Mile in Brussels' Heysel Stadium was the setting for the third record in nine days.

Tom Byers set the pace in the first lap, and soon there were just three men who anyone had eyes for; Byers, Coe and veteran Kenyan Mike Boit. With 500 metres to go Byers was done, and although Boit set a new African record of 3:49.45, he was more than 15 metres down on Coe, who destroyed the old record and clocked 3:47.33... more than a second lower than Ovett's best, and a mark which would last until after the next Olympic Games, when a third Briton of this era would make his mark.

The greatness of Coe and Ovett can never be disputed, and after this golden summer for the mile each enjoyed some highs but also various lows in the rest of their athletics careers.

In the 1984 Olympics in Los Angeles finished second in the 800 metres final to Brazil's Joaquim Cruz, but memorably retained his 1500 metres title in 3:32.53, ahead of world champion Steve Cram. Ovett dropped out on the final lap suffering from a chest infection. Two years later, at the European Championships in Stuttgart, Coe won the 800 metres in a British clean sweep ahead of Tom McKean and Cram, but Coe never had the chance for a third Olympic 1500 metres gold, as he was not selected for the Seoul games after failing in the British trials through illness.

Now Lord Coe, he has gone on to a career in politics as a Conservative MP, as well as leading the British bid, and organisation, of the 2012 Olympic Games in London.

Ovett's 1982 season was massively disrupted by a training injury in which he slipped and impaled his thigh on church railings, but he came back the following summer to finish fourth in the 1500 metres at the first World Championship in Helsinki, then on September 4 took the 1500 metres world record to 3:30.77 in Rieti.

However, 1984 was a horrible year, and he defied medical advice to run both the 800 metres and 1500 at Los Angeles, finishing last in the 800 final, and stepping out on the last lap of the 1500 metres as Coe swept to glory – Ovett's race ending in the arms of the medics.

Ovett took gold at the Edinburgh Commonwealth Games of 1986, leading an English clean sweep of the 5000 metres ahead of Jack Buckner and Tim Hutching, but the longer distances were not really for him.

After retiring from athletics, he moved to Australia.

In his revealing 2012 interview with Mike Walters in the *Daily Mirror*, Ovett said: "Our rivalry was a great thing for the sport, but it was largely a media invention. Do we swap Christmas cards? Actually, yes we do – and nor were we sworn enemies off the track. The reality is that it suited both of us to be cast as arch-rivals. He was portrayed as the posh boy and I was supposedly the rough diamond, but when you stripped away the lacquers that were layered over the truth, we were, and are, very similar characters.

"Seb's route to achieving things was different to mine – his background was in indoor racing, mine was in cross-country, he became a peer of the realm while I ended up living in Australia, and you can't live another man's life. But, hey, you couldn't have written the script better. We were two guys from totally different backgrounds, from the same country, in the same era, chasing the same dreams.

"At one stage, before times were measured in hundredths of a second, we even held the same world record for 1500 metres. That's how closely matched we were, and if you wanted to cultivate a rivalry, it was too good to be true."

The last 'golden hurrah' for British mile running came with the golden haired runner who followed in the immediate aftermath of Coe and Ovett, who had been forged by competition against those two greats, who had trailed in their wake… but who was already starting to overtake them as their careers ebbed slightly. ➤

> "Seb's route was different to mine – he became a peer of the realm while I ended up living in Australia. But, hey, you couldn't have written the script better."

ABOVE LEFT: Sebastian Coe sprints clear of Steve Cram to win 1500 metres gold at Los Angeles.

ABOVE: Coe gestures to the press box after that 1984 win, as some journalists had criticised the decision to select him for the Olympic team.

BELOW LEFT: Arrogant or just very proud? Steve Ovett of Great Britain celebrated in style after winning his 800 metres gold in Moscow.

BELOW: A dejected Ovett struggled with injury at many major games in the mid 1980s, unable to produce his best form.

FOUR MINUTE MILE 105

Born in England's North East in 1960, the 'Jarrow arrow' was a youngster with massive potential and was selected for the 1980 Olympics as a 19-year-old after beating Graham Williamson in a run-off.

He had joined Jarrow & Hebburn Athletics Club when aged 12 and just two years later was fourth in the 1500 metres at the English Schools Championship. By 1978 he set a world age-17 mile best ran for England at the Commonwealth Games in Edmonton, Canada.

In that first Olympic final he came in last, but it had been an important learning experience for Cram and just two years later he came to the fore – perhaps helped by health problems for both Coe and Ovett – when he won the 1500 metres at both the European Championships – in 3:36.49 – and then the Commonwealth Games, beating John Walker in 3:42.37 to the New Zealander's 3:43.11.

That same year Cram broke his first world record as part of the British team which ran 7:03.89 for the 4 x 800 metres at Crystal Palace; he was on the third leg, following on from Peter Elliott, Garry Cook and handing over to Coe.

His major breakthrough came in 1983 at the first World Championships in Helsinki, when he won the 1500 metres. In a fantastic race, Morocco's Said Aouita made a break with 500 to go, Cram went with him and inside the last 200 strode away to win in 3:41.59 with Steve Scott second in 3:41.87 and Aouita third in 3:42.02, just ahead of Ovett.

Cram's greatest season on the record-breaking front came in 1985, and that's when he enters our mile pantheon of greats. Coe had broken three world records in 41 days in 1981, however, Cram did the same thing in just 19.

His rivalry with Aouita was thrilling the athletics world and at Nice on July 16 both men became the first to break 3:30 for 1500 metres, Cram winning in 3:29.67, just four hundredths ahead of his rival, then 11 days later, in Oslo – scene of so many records – he took Coe's mile record in 3:46.32, a mark which would stand for

ABOVE: Silver and gold... Sebastian Coe and Steve Cram took the top two places in the 1984 Olympic 1500 metres.

LEFT: A third rival was on the scene in the early 1980s, and at the 1983 World Championship Steve Cram held off Morocco's Said Aouita, American Steve Scott and Steve Ovett to win.

RIGHT: Masterclass... Steve Cram had some great domestic examples to try and emulate, and was part of the 4 x 800 metres relay team which broke a world record.

eight years, before, on August 4, he added the 2000 metres best in 4:51.39.

But for our purposes it was that Dream Mile event at the Bislett Games which was most dramatic, as he beat Coe and a host of others to enter the history books.

American James Mays took the race out, with Australian Mike Hillardt and Coe hard behind alongside Jose-Luis Gonzalez, Scott and Cram, moving very easily. At the halfway point it was 1:53.82 and as Mays faded Hillardt took over, with the runners eyeing each other, unsure as to who was most danger – Cram with his long run for home or Coe with his devastating final kick.

But Cram's strategy was to leave it later than many predicted, a 1000 metres race having given him confidence as he'd blitzed he final 200 of that in 24.4. "That was a crucial race," he later said. "It gave me a great mental lift. Everybody would be writing that I'd go from the bell, but I knew that with Coe there, I had to have that reserve for the last 200."

With a lap to go the time was showing 2:53. "I thought, this is not going to be a record," said Cram. But then shortly into the final lap the race exploded into action, Cram accelerating with Coe and Gonzalez trying to stay with him. Cram later said he was convinced Coe was struggling ever so slightly… so gave it absolutely everything.

He moved ahead around the final bend and crossed the line in 3:46.32, more than a second faster than Coe's old record. Gonzalez overtook Coe for second in 3:47.79 to the Olympic 1500 metres champion's 3:49.22, while Scott came home in 3:49.93.

It was the last time – at time of writing – a Briton would hold the mile world record, and it had been done in a proper 'race', not a time trial, but a battle between men determined to win.

Cram's career wasn't quite over, the following year he won the Commonwealth Games 800 and 1500 metres double in Edinburgh, while at the European Championships he finished third in the 800 metres, but retained his 1500 metres title, at last beating Coe in a major championship.

Troubled by injury after that, he was disappointing at the Seoul Olympics, and again in 1990 he finished fifth in the 1500 metres after another disrupted season.

Now forging a career as a television commentator, many younger viewers may not quite appreciate how great a runner the man behind the microphone was… the third piece in Britain's great middle distance triumvirate of the 1970s and 80s.

The mile record would remain in Cram's possession for eight years, until the appearance of the second African to lower the mark. ■

LEFT: Post athletics, Steve Cram has forged a career as a TV commentator, but the 'Jarrow arrow' still holds the British mile record.

BELOW: Steve Cram didn't just follow in Coe and Ovett's wake, he could beat them when all were at their peak, such as this 1983 mile race with Steve Ovett.

SOMALIA
Atlanta 1996
2208
adidas
ALGERI
Atlanta
1012
adidas

Out of Africa...
and over the horizon?

If the Olympic 1500 metre title is 'first cousin' to the world mile record, it was clear from looking at the medal table towards the end of the 20th century where the balance of power in the middle distance running 'family' was shifting.

Sebastian Coe and Steve Cram's British one-two at Los Angeles in 1984 was followed up by the silver medal of Peter Elliott at Seoul in 1988, but at those games the Rotherham man was beaten to the line by Kenyan Peter Rono. He was the second man from Africa to be crowned Olympic champion – Kip Keino having triumphed at altitude versus Jim Ryun in Mexico – but it was a clear indication that this continent was a growing force at the middle distances.

Spain's Fermin Cacho won on home ground at Barcelona in 1992, outsprinting his rivals following a fairly pedestrian race and delighting the partisan crowd, but since then the list of nations having won Olympic gold at the distance reads: Algeria, Kenya, Morocco, Kenya and Algeria (the current champion being Taoufik Makhloufi).

And two of those winners are the final two men (so far) to register on the list of mile world record holders – Noureddine Morceli and a man considered perhaps the greatest middle distance runner yet, Hicham El Guerrouj.

Algeria's Morceli was born in 1970 in Ténès, and was a top-rank junior, taking silver in the 1500 metres at the World Junior Championships in 1988. Coached by his older brother Abderrahmane, who competed in the 1980 and 1984 Olympics Algeria in the Moscow Olympics of 1980 and in Los Angeles in 1984, he immediately made a mark at senior level, setting a 1990 season's best of 3:37.87 in the 1500 metres, and continued to impress through the following year both indoors and out, breaking the 1500 world indoor record for at Seville on February 28, his 21st birthday. Just over a week later he became world indoor champion, and throughout the outdoor season he was undefeated at the distance, winning the world title in Tokyo in a time of 3:32.84, well ahead of second-placed Wilfred Kirochi of Kenya.

Early in 1992 Morceli set a new 1000 metres indoor world record of 2:15.26 and he looked to be the man to beat at Barcelona, but was there a weakness… could he be out-kicked for glory? He had been struggling with a hip injury and before the games Morceli was beaten by the often under-rated Italian Gennaro di Napoli in Rome, while Kenyan David Kibet beat him in that summer's Oslo Dream Mile.

Morceli qualified well for the final, but in that race the pace was woefully slow, the field passing through the 800 metres mark in a slower time than in the women's final. With no one taking the race on, it became a competition for the sprinters, and Morceli was never in the frame, coming home seventh. ➤

FAR LEFT: Algeria's Noureddine Morceli emerged as the man who could take Steve Cram's world mile best, then added medals to his haul of honours.

ABOVE LEFT: In the same year as he broke the mile record, Morceli defeated Ireland's Marcus O'Sullivan to win the Wanamaker Mile in New York.

ABOVE: But just as Morceli seemed in control, the rising force emerged as Hicham El Guerrouj... and the two would enjoy a great on-track rivalry.

BELOW & RIGHT: Kenya's Noah Ngeny won the 1500 metres gold at Sydney in 2000, leaving El Guerrouj devastated.

RIGHT: The Moroccan bounced back four years later to take gold.

The Algerian clearly needed a stronger pace throughout in order to assert his authority, and he proved he was in shape just days after the Olympics when he set a season's best 1500 metres time in Monaco, then the following week ran a personal best 3:30.76 in Zurich. The inevitable happened on September 6, when he finally took Said Aouita's seven-year-old world record in a race at Rieti, coming home in 3:28.

Morceli was dominant, but there was one record he wanted... Steve Cram's mile best which had stood defiant since July 1985.

Throughout 1993 he added more titles and records – Mediterranean Games gold World Championship gold – and in late summer was in fantastic shape, twice narrowly missing Cram's record in Berlin and Brussels, running the fifth and third fastest miles in those two events.

Eamonn Coghlan – whose world indoor mile best Morceli had been aiming to annexe – remarked at the time that the Algerian's strength was just as much mental as physical: "He runs with no fear," Coghlan said. "Runners in the western world have a tendency to create psychological barriers for themselves. He runs at will, with no inhibitions."

Two days after that Belgian attempt, and 24 hours short of a year after taking the 1500 metres world record, he again travelled to Rieti for a performance which sent shock waves through athletics... he didn't just beat Cram's best, he destroyed it, as in bettering Cram's mark by 1.93 seconds, the 23-year-old produced the biggest drop in the record in 28 years. The new mark stood at 3:44.39.

"I'd been close three times this season, but never had good atmospheric conditions," he said afterwards.

Pacemakers took Morceli through the first 1200 metres, then it was down to him... and the crowd which chanted his name throughout the attempt. No one was close to him at the end, with second-placed Venuste Nyongabo of Burundi finishing in 3:55.86, and Ahmed Ibrahim of Qatar even further back and crossing the line in 3:57.58.

Were we witnessing the greatest middle distance runner ever? As always, just as in the days of George,

ABOVE: El Guerrouj's dreams shattered in 1996 when he fell during the 1500 metres final, but a call from the king helped restore his determination.

Nuurmi, Lovelock, Ryun and Coe, just when you think the best ever has arrived, someone comes along to challenge and take the mantle onwards… but not quite yet, there was still life in Morceli, and some glory days to come.

His success continued into 1994 when he set a new 3000 metres world record (7:25.11), and also enjoyed victories at 5000 metres. The only defeat of his season came during an 800 metres race in Cologne.

The next year – 1995 – he broke the 2000 metre world best and in early July set the last world record of his career, lowered his own 1500 metres record to 3:27.37, before going on to claim the world title over the same distance.

But that rising rival was snapping at his heels, and when in 1996 Morceli set a world season's best of 3:29.50, not long after Hicham El Guerrouj won in Hengelo in a time just one hundredth of a second slower. At the Atlanta Olympics it was a straight battle between the two… but when El Guerrouj fell on the last lap, Morceli took immediate tactical advantage and accelerated away, to eventually finish five metres clear of defending champion Fermin Cacho, who had to avoid his fallen opponent.

Later in 1996 Morceli was beaten by Morocco's El Guerrouj in a 1500 metre race in Milan. The torch had passed onto the next great middle distance star… the man who still (well… at time of writing) holds both mile and 1500 metres world records.

Hicham El Guerrouj announced himself on the world stage in 1992 when, aged just 18, he was third in the 5000 metres of the Junior World Championships in Seoul. By 1994 he was a member of the Moroccan team in the IAAF World Road Relay Championships, a group which won the race in world record time, and the following year, when still just 20, he finished runner-up in the 1500 metres to Noureddine Morceli at the 1995 World Championships in Gothenburg.

Going into 1996, his was the name on everyone's lips, especially after lowering his personal best time ▶

> *"(Morceli) runs with no fear. Runners in the West have a tendency to create psychological barriers for themselves."*

Hicham El Guerrouj has enjoyed massive success on the track, both in winning medals, but also breaking records. He currently holds the world bests indoors and outdoors at both the mile and 1500 metres.
Here (**LEFT & BELOW**) he celebrates Olympic gold in 2004, while (**RIGHT**) it's world gold in 1999... and also victory in the Emsley Carr Mile in 2000 (**BELOW RIGHT**).

over 1500 metres to 3:29.59 in Stockholm, and this North African sensation was considered one of the favourites for the Olympic gold.

At those Atlanta games it all went horribly wrong when, moving into position to challenge for the lead with just over a lap to go, El Guerrouj fell. World record holder Noureddine Morceli disappeared into the distance to take gold. After the race, the distraught Moroccan received a phone call from Moroccan head of state King Hassan, who told El Guerrouj that he was convinced better times lay ahead for the athlete.

"After the call by His Majesty, it was another El Guerrouj who was born," he later said. "There is no similarity to the El Guerrouj before that call and El Guerrouj now."

Just a month later, at the Grand Prix final in Milan, El Guerrouj became the first man in four years to defeat Morceli over 1500 metres.

He began to dominate, and in 1997 set two world indoor records, starting with a 1500 metres best of 3:31.18 (eclipsing Morceli's previous time) and then finally claiming Eamonn Coghlan's 14-year-old mile record by running 3:48.45.

The following year his dominance continued, and in Rome that July he took more than a second off Morceli's 1500 metres world record with a time of 3:26.00, helped by a teenage Kenyan pacemaker called Noah Ngeny.

Finally, and most importantly as far as this publication is concerned, the Eternal City saw a lowering of the mile record by another significant margin... a record which, at time of going to press, has stood for almost 15 years.

El Guerrouj again targeted Rome's Olympic Stadium as the site of his record attempt on the mile. A $50,000 prize was on offer if anyone broke the record, and a quality field was on hand to make a race of it... but surely there was just one man with a realistic chance?

Former Olympic 800 metre champion William Tanui took the pace on early, with El Guerrouj and Ngeny – this time in there as a competitor rather than a 'rabbit' – tucked in behind. The first lap took just 55.07 seconds and the half mile 1:51.58... this was a serious pace and there were just the three men in the frame – El Guerrouj, Ngeny and his fellow Kenyan Tanui leading the way.

At the bell it was 2:47.91... and then there were two, as Tanui stepped away.

This final lap had something which Bannister could only have dreamed of all those years before, the 'giant screen' in the corner, which allowed El Guerrouj to see the position of his opponent, a man he perhaps hadn't expected to be within a stride of him, but who was now turning this into a race.

The two were giving no quarter, and around the final bend the Kenyan was just two strides behind El Guerrouj and Ngeny moved slightly wider to try and overtake... but again, El Guerrouj could see the move coming thanks to the screen, and he battled on, remaining just an agonising stride or two ahead of Ngeny all the way to the line.

The race was won... but what about the time? Had Morceli's record survived?

This wasn't 1954, thanks to the wonders of instant replays men with stopwatches and overcoats weren't the arbiters, and the clock showed a fantastic new world best, indeed both men had trounced the previous world record.

El Guerrouj crossed the line in 3:43.13, a time which survives to this day, while Ngeny's 3:43.40 also eclipsed Morceli's mark – he hadn't previously broken 3:50. It was the first time two men had broken the mile record in the same race since 1958, when Herb Elliott and Merv Lincoln had beaten Derek Ibbotson's time.

El Guerrouj was ecstatic, but also delighted to see one of his heroes conducting interviews for the BBC, and greeted Steve Cram with a huge hug. "My favorite mile race was when Cram beat Coe in Oslo (in 1985) – that was a great race," said El Guerrouj, a keen student of his sport, and a man never afraid to race.

Later that year El Guerrouj set a new world record over 2000 metres in Berlin at 4:44.79, bettering Morceli's previous record by more than three seconds, and his tag as favourite for the 1500 metres at Sydney's Olympics in 2000 seemed fully justified. But Ngeny produced a great performance to take that title ahead of El Guerrouj and third-placed Bernard Lagat.

As far as the mile is concerned, the story is over... at least for now. But the man who holds the record enjoyed considerable further success before retiring from the sport. El Guerrouj defended his 1500 metres title in both 2001 and 2003, won three consecutive IAAF Golden League prizes – in 2001, 2002 and 2003, while in that latter year also set a personal best in the 5000 metres of 12:50.24 before going on to claim silver at the world championships in that longer distance.

His decade at the top was coming to an end, but could he go out on a high at the 2004 Athens Olympics?

A quiet start to the season suggested it may be one championships too far, and just three weeks before the games he lost narrowly to Lagat at the Weltklasse meeting in Zurich. But those two would produce a great Olympic 1500 metres final as round the final bend El Guerrouj held a narrow lead before Lagat edged in front. But the Moroccan would not be denied, and showed he was a supreme competitor as well as record breaker when he fought on to re-take the lead just yards from the line.

Four days later El Guerrouj won the 5000 metres final, becoming the first man since Paavo Nurmi 80 years earlier to win both 1500 and 5000 metre titles in the same games.

For the mile... perhaps we really have reached the peak, and the man who holds the record now is truly a special athlete, being the first (and so far only) man to hold all four 'mile' titles – metric and imperial – by being best indoors and outdoors at the mile and also the 1500 metres. ∎

ABOVE & ABOVE LEFT: In familiar pose, Hicham El Guerrouj celebrates winning 1999 world championship gold and the Olympic 5000 metres gold medal in 2004.

An exclusive club

From lords of the land to knights of the realm, captains of industry to national and sporting ambassadors, the men who are in the exclusive club of having held the world mile record have led varied lives since retiring from athletics.

What they seem to have in common, and perhaps what the discipline of succeeding at this particular event gives, is an ability to achieve in other spheres too. And perhaps none more so that the first man to hold the sub-four record, Dr Roger Bannister.

Because the man with the elegant stride and scientific approach to his training is far more proud of his achievements away from the athletics track than those on the cinders, as remarkable as they were. His brief athletics career at the very top – fourth in the Olympics of 1952, European and Empire champion in 1954, world record holder for just over one month from May 1954 – may not stack up on the statistics front with the likes of El Guerrouj, a personable star athlete who certainly knows his sporting history – but for Bannister it was a fantastic thing to do before the rest of his life kicked in.

When asked a decade ago whether the sub-four mile was his most important achievement, Bannister replied that it was not... and that his subsequent distinguished medical career, as well as his time as master of Pembroke College and chairman of the Sports Council, were far more satisfying.

As Bannister said in 2000: "My core, my whole life was medicine. I wanted to become a specialist. It took 10 years to become a consultant in neurology. Alongside my neurology, I have always had some public involvement in sports and sports promotion."

John Landy's career post athletics was another which has involved business success as well as public service, working in senior positions at ICI Australia, serving on the Land Conservation Council of Victoria, and most famously becoming the 26th Governor of the state of Victoria. Showered with accolades and honorary degrees, the 84-year-old will go down in history as one of the great sportsmen in the true sense of the word.

Derek Ibbotson's career after athletics was another which was rich and varied, the Yorkshireman working for a top sportswear firm in design and product development, while he also helped Manchester City FC win the League Championship, acting as fitness coach at the club during the team's run of success in the late 1960s. He was awarded the MBE for services to athletics in 2008.

ABOVE: John Walker has served as a councillor in his native New Zealand, while Seb Coe (**BELOW & BELOW LEFT**) has received many honours, and led London's 2012 Olympic bid.

Herb Elliott was another who enjoyed a successful business career Down Under, most notably with Fortescue Metals, while Sir Peter Snell, now aged 75, moved to the US in the early 1970s, gained a PhD and enjoyed a rich and varied career, which included becoming a champion orienteer.

Politics has famously been a major part of many of the record holders' lives – Jim Ryun was elected as a Republican member of the US House of Representatives from 1996 to 2007, Sir John Walker is an independant city councillor in his native New Zealand, as well as running an equestrian shop in Auckland with his wife, while most famously of all to UK readers will be Lord Sebastian Coe's political career. He was elected as a Conservative MP for Falmouth from 1992 to 1997, but was defeated in that year's general election when Tony Blair's Labour swept to power, then became chief of staff to Tory leader William Hague for a short while, having been given a life peerage in 2000. Coe took over from Barbara Cassani as chairman of London's Olympic bid for the 2012 games, and helped provide a spectacular games in the UK capital, before moving on to become chairman of the British Olympic Association.

Steve Cram's post athletics career has also been high profile, working as a commentator on athletics for the BBC, as well as covering the Winter Olympics of 2014, while Steve Ovett has kept a relatively far lower profile, having moved to Australia.

Current world record holder Hicham El Guerrouj – a hero in his homeland – is still forging a post-athletics career, and among many roles is a Unicef Goodwill Ambassador.

The post career roles are as varied and interesting as the men who have graced that list of mile record holders…∎

ABOVE: Steve Cram held the Olympic torch in his native North East in 2012 and is now a TV presenter.

BELOW: Jim Ryun was elected to office in the US.

Women going hell for Leather

Just over three weeks after Roger Bannister ran the first sub-four minute mile, a woman from the West Midlands broke another significant barrier. Mention her to the wider public and it's only the sport's aficionados among them who will recognise the name Diane Leather... but that perhaps says much for the inequities in the sporting arena.

This publication has focused on the fastest human over one mile, and all that time it's been a man who held the record, whether from Europe, North America, Australasia or Africa. We have focused on the characters, the results, the times and the races involving those fastest humans over 1760 yards, and celebrated the 60th anniversary of Bannister's efforts.

But there have been many superb women athletes struggling for recognition, and they are worthy of books and magazines on their own. These following pages will pay respect to just a few of the achievements of a succession of top quality runners in what should perhaps be seen as a separate event, a race in which no comparison can ever be direct... so is perhaps best not attempted.

With athletics very much being a sport of statistics, it's strange to reflect that the time recorded by current women's mile record holder, Svetlana Masterkova, 4:12.56, is effectively the same as that run by the first man to have beaten Walter George's 19th century time – Norman Taber's record of 1915.

But in May 1954 a Briton finally broke through a significant 'barrier', and her name was Diane Leather, the first woman to run a mile in less than five minutes.

If the woman from Staffordshire had been a competitor these days, Leather, or Diane Charles as she became after her marriage, would have been a star, perhaps an Olympic champion... perhaps a Dame.

But during her career there was no Olympic event for women that was longer than 200 metres, and world records only went up to 800 metres and 880 yards.

As a result of this, the nearest time to a mile you'll see Leather's name on the official world record lists is when she ran 2:09.0 for the half-mile on June 19, 1954. And that was while she was in a rich vein of record-breaking form.

Leather – who apparently only started running to improve her fitness for hockey – first broke the unofficial mile world record in 1953 when she recorded a time of 5:02.6, and she improved this to 5:00.2 on May 26, 1954. Just three days later, and 23 days after Bannister, Chataway and Brasher created history in Oxford, she clocked 4:59.6 in a race at the Midland Championships in Birmingham.

And there was plenty more to come, as she broke the record on two other occasions, stopping the clock at 4:50.8 in May 1955, then 4:45.0 that September.

In the metric event, she broke the 1500 metres world record twice in 1957, recording 4:30.0 at

Diane Leather was ahead of the field for much of the 1950s, but her records were never given the recognition they deserved.

Hornchurch in May, and 4:29.7 in London the following month. But she was past her best when the chance came to run in the Olympics at her better distances. Although she had taken silver in the 800 metres at the 1954 and 1958 European Championships, the 1960 Olympics came just that year or two too late for her, and running as Diane Charles she was knocked out in the first round of the 800 metres.

She had enjoyed a great career, but one which would have gained so much more recognition if she'd been born just a few decades later and she'd been able to show the world her ability at her favoured distance.

The dominant figure in her chosen events, Leather won five WAAA titles between 1954 and 1957 and the national cross-country title between 1953 and 1956.

Leather's mile world best remained the time to beat for several years but was finally broken in Perth by New Zealand's Marise Chamberlain, who ran 4:41.4 in 1962.

The talented Chamberlain set world records at 440 yards, the half-mile and the mile, taking a silver at the 1962 Empire and Commonwealth Games at 880 yards, and at the 1964 Olympics won a bronze at the event behind Ann Packer and Maryvonne Dupureur.

Apart from her mile best, she's also best remembered for an athletics heartbreak, as while leading the Empire and Commonwealth 880 yards final, she stumbled close to the finish and ended up missing out on the medals.

This chapter won't simply list all the women who have held the mile record, there are other publications which can do that in far more depth, but there are significant moments and 'mileposts' along the way which can and should be highlighted, such as the efforts of the woman who relieved Chamberlain of her record.

Anne Rosemary Smith, a talented runner from Amersham who was coached by Gordon Pirie, broke two world records in one race at Chiswick in June 1967, running 4:17.3 for the 1500 metres and then going on to cross the line for the mile in 4:37.0 for the mile. She had already broken the mile record the month before, but this second lowering of the mark was the first time the record was ratified by the IAAF.

Smith went on to become a PE teacher, but died at the tragically young age of 52 in 1993 following a brain haemorrhage.

Europeans Mia Gommers, Ellen Tittel and Paola Pigni lowered the record over the next decade, then from 1977 the record bounced between the United States and Eastern Europe… or rather, between one American athlete who would become notorious in the UK for one racing incident, and a series of runners from Romania and Russia/USSR.

Italy's Pigni had taken the record below 4.30 in August 1973, then the first of those Romanians, Natalia Marasescu, took over as record holder first by running 4:23.8 in Bucharest, then lowering that in January 1979 in Auckland.

She will always be tainted by the shadow of doping, as the Romanian was banned for taking anabolic steroids in 1979 for 18 months, even though after just eight months Marasescu was reinstated following IAAF president Adriaan Paulen's claim that the lengthy ban, which would have kept her out of the Moscow Olympics, meant "an extra penalty". ▶

> "She enjoyed a great career, but would have gained so much more recognition if she'd been born just a few decades later and she'd been able to show the world her ability."

Diane Leather attracted plenty of press attention following her sub-five run, but together with Roger Bannister continues to inspire future generations.

FOUR MINUTE MILE 117

However, when it came to 'not going to the Olympics', the next holder of the mile record seemed to have cornered the market in methods of not becoming an Olympian, even though by the Moscow Games she had taken the mile world record having beaten the previous record in January 1980.

Mary Decker dominates the next decade of women's middle distance running, but was already a star in her native United States by the time the 1980s started.

The only woman to have held both indoor and outdoor world mile records was born in New Jersey in 1958, and 10 years later her family moved to California, where the youngster started running, and seemingly became obsessed with the sport.

Aged just 12, in one week she ran a marathon, four other middle and longer distance races, then ended the week with an appendectomy.

Within a couple of years she was international class, but couldn't go to the Munich Olympics of 1972 as she was too young at just 14, even though by the end of 1972 she was ranked fourth in the world at 800 metres, while in 1973 she gained her first world record, running an indoor mile in 4:40.1.

But the next phase of her career would be dominated by injury, perhaps brought on by the massive amount of running she was doing at such a young age. Stress fractures of her lower leg kept her out of the 1976 Olympics, while in 1978 she had an operation to try and cure the compartment syndrome from which she'd been suffering. In 1979 she became the second American woman (after Francie Larrieu) to break 4:30 for the mile then after already breaking the mile best in Auckland in January 1980, she ran 4:17.55... however, this time was never ratified by the IAAF.

Decker was unable to run in the 1980 Olympics due to the boycott, then the Russian athlete Lyudmila Veselkova took the official record in September 1981 when she ran 4:20.89, but the now-married Decker-Tabb bounced back with 4:18.08 in 1982 in Paris, the first time the 4:20 barrier had officially been broken, and part of a memorable year during which she took six world records.

ABOVE: A young Decker proved that women have the pace to eventually crack four minutes for a mile. In 1978, while a student at the University of Colorado, she won the women's half-mile in San Diego with a time of 2:03.5. She had hoped to crack the two minute mark at that meeting.

RIGHT: American Mary Decker was a confirmed front runner, and she struck double gold at the first World Championships in Helsinki in 1983.

Her mile record would only last a few months though, as Romania's Maricica Puica lowered the record in the September during a race in Rieti.

The first World Championships in Helsinki in 1983 saw her achieve double gold with the 1500 and 3000 metres titles, then the following year saw the incident for which most Britons will remember her, the 3000 metres 'clash' with Zola Budd, the South African-born British runner who still holds the British mile best.

Decker, who had divorced in 1983 and was now the girlfriend of British discus thrower Richard Slaney, clipped the heel of Budd in the final and fell, failing to finish. Puica went on to take gold, Britain's Wendy Sly coming second and Budd was initially disqualified after running on and crossing the line seventh, but was then later reinstated after officials watched the incident again. Decker was the golden girl at her home Olympics, her dream was shattered and her claims that Budd had bumped into her and cost her gold were supported by the American press, and Budd was hounded by reporters.

> "Some people think she tripped me deliberately. I know that wasn't the case. I fell because I am, and was, inexperienced in running in a pack."

Years later, Decker-Slaney (who had by now married the Briton) said: "The reason I fell, some people think she tripped me deliberately. I happen to know that wasn't the case at all. The reason I fell is because I am and was very inexperienced in running in a pack."

Decker-Slaney went on to have a great 1985, dominating the European circuit, and set a new official world record for the women's mile of 4:16.71 in Zurich in the August.

An unratified record had been set the year before by the Soviet Union's Natalia Artymove, unofficial because the timing for the race, won in 4:15.8, had been manual hand-held, and thus unrecognised by the governing body. ➤

ABOVE & BELOW: Mary Decker was the dominant figure over more than a decade-and-a-half in women's mile running, but her most infamous moment came over the longer 3000 metres at Los Angeles, when her collision with Zola Budd sent the American sprawling on the track.

FOUR MINUTE MILE 119

The 'official' Decker-Slaney record was billed as a rematch after 'The Fall' by the US media, as official mile world record holder Puica, who had also won that 3000 gold Decker-Slaney felt was hers, was the other fancied runner.

American Diana Richburg set the early pace but dropped out with two laps to go, then Decker-Slaney, an experienced front runner – mainly because she had been in a class of her own in the States so often simply had to run on her own – took it on.

Puica stuck to her task and desperately tried to overtake on the home straight, but the American held her off to take back her record, even though Puica came inside her old record, setting a new European best in the process at 4:17.33, while third-placed Zola Budd, running barefoot, set a British record of 4:17.57.

Decker-Slaney's mark would stand for four years, but her career as an athlete would carry on and, typical for her, included many more controversies.

After becoming a mother in 1986, and missing the following year through injury, she had a disappointing Seoul Olympics, did not qualify for Barcelona in 1992, but qualified for Atlanta 1996 in the 5000 metres, where the by-now 37-year-old was eliminated in the heats, but not before a drugs controversy, when she failed a test but then launched a series of appeals as her legal team argued the test was unreliable for women in their late 30s who were taking birth control pills.

Her career blighted by stress fractures of her legs, she retired to a ranch in Oregon, but her competitive streak remains, and she competes in the ElliptiGO world championships, using the low-impact bicycle.

The woman who broke Decker-Slaney's record enjoyed a golden period of domination in women's middle distance running in the late 1980s.

ABOVE & RIGHT: Svetlana Masterkova's greatest results came after she became a mother and following a terrible run of injuries. Another confirmed front runner, she took titles and records by taking the lead... and staying there.

FAR RIGHT: The powerful Paula Ivan followed a great tradition of Romanian milers when she broke Mary Decker's record in July 1989.

She was another Romanian, Paula Ivan, and in July 1989 the Olympic 1500 metres champion and 3000 metres silver medal winner shattered the previous record during a race at Nice.

Just 10 days before Ivan's 26th birthday, her compatriot Violeta Beclea led the field to halfway before stepping out to leave Ivan, and another Romanian, the 1984 Olympic 1500 metres champion Doina Melinte, to battle it out. Ivan pushed the pace to move well clear of her veteran opponent, and finished 30 yards clear to knock more than a second off the record time and lower it to 4:15.61.

After a golden 1989, during which she also won the Universiade and also the 1500 metres at the IAAF World Cup, she then retired to become a coach. However, after a decade out she returned for one last season on the European circuit in 2000.

By then, she was no longer world mile record holder, as that title had gone to the woman who possesses the record to this day... and who took the record in the first mile she had ever raced.

Svetlana Masterkova was born in 1968 in Russia, and although she became national champion at 800 metres in 1991, and competed in the world championships, it was only after an enforced break of a couple of seasons due to injuries and then the birth of her daughter, that she became a phenomenon.

In 1996 she returned to the top level and decided to run 1500 metres as well as 800, but was not considered a favourite for the Atlanta Olympics as Maria Mutola and Ana Quirot were heavily backed to land the gold and silver in the 800 metres. The Russian surprised them all though by hitting the front early... and staying there, running away from the field to become champion. She then stunned the world by doing exactly the same thing in the 1500 metres.

But Masterkova's stunning summer continued, and at the Weltklasse Grand Prix meeting at Zurich on August 14 she utterly destroyed the previous record of Paula Ivan, taking the new mark down to 4:12.56.

In her usual style Masterkova led all the way, beating runner-up Regina Jacobs of the United States by more than nine seconds and it was equally stunning because it was the first mile she had ever raced, and came just 18 months after giving birth.

"I knew when I was carrying the baby I wanted to get back to running, and I did in two months," Masterkova said. "Before the race, I didn't think I would run that fast. However, Ludmilla (Borisova, the pacemaker) did a perfect pacing job."

The record holder suffered a frustrating 1997 due to an Achilles injury, but was back on form again in 1998, becoming European champion at 1500 metres, while at the 1999 world championships she could only win bronze in the 800 metres, but bounced back to claim gold in the 1500.

The Sydney Olympics was her last hurrah, and she suffered frustration in the 1500 metres, stepping out of her heat, and retired at the end of that season.

Just like the men's world record, the women's version is 'stuck' in the 20th century... only time will tell if an athlete of good enough quality can take it forward again. The sport has often been hit by doping controversies, and there will always be suspicion over some of the records set during the Cold War era. The fact the women's 1500 metres title has remained the possession of China's Qu Yunxia for more than 20 years, suggests it could be a while yet before the mile best comes under threat. ∎

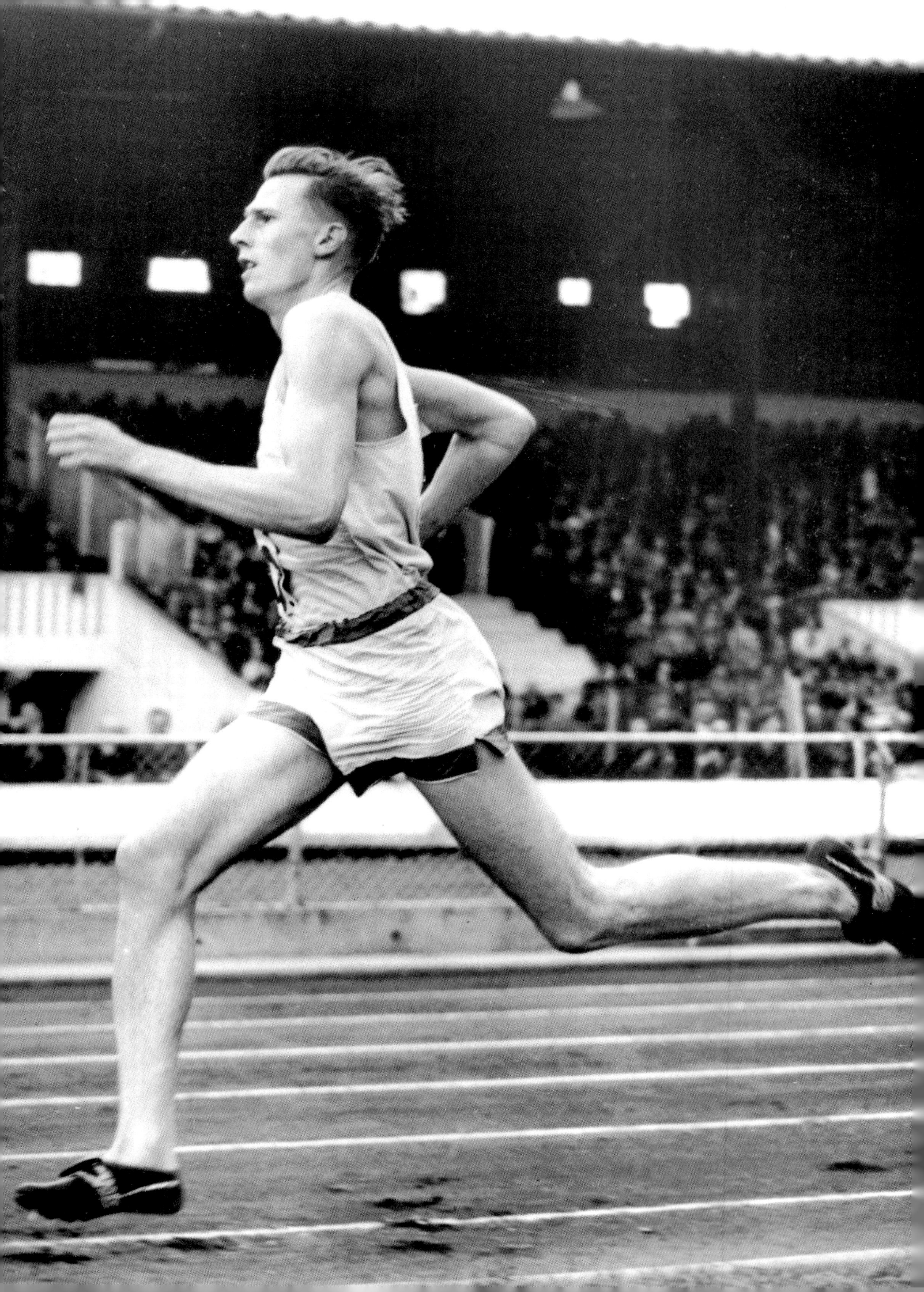

The last lap

So what is it about the mile that has held such a special place in the heart of so many? What significance does and can Roger Bannister's achievements six decades ago really have now in the 21st century?

What's clear is that top-class milers know and respect their history, know their event, and respect the men who went before them. As Eamonn Coghlan told the author: "The mile is very much about tradition, but it's also an easy race to understand, as is the significance of running sub-four minutes... it's four laps all in approximately 60 seconds – or less.

"Mankind understands the challenge, and even now after all this time it's a respected mark to hit. People do run the event less frequently these days, the 1500 metres is more popular and there's fewer mile events on the TV. But the public are clued in about it, and for them and participants a sub-four is still special, it lets an athlete know where they are," added the Irish athletics legend.

Matthew Fraser Moat, race organiser with the British Milers' Club, an organisation which bills itself as the premier middle distance athletics club in the country, uses a word which many others have linked to this distance – 'symmetry'.

"The thing about the four minute mile is the symmetry. Four laps of the track in four minutes. Most club athletes can get close to running a lap in a minute, good club athletes can run two laps of the track in two minutes... but to run four laps in four minutes is exceptional, and it remains an exceptional performance today some 60 years after Sir Roger's great achievement in 1954," he said.

"It is always a magic moment to hear the announcer start the results by saying "and the winning time is, three minutes...", and I have had the honour to have organised three races where a sub four minute mile has been set."

Statistician and author Bob Phillips is convinced the number of people who would have run the sub-four mile would be three or four times higher were it not for the fact that 1500 metres is the standard distance in athletics competition these days and the mile is run ➤

ABOVE: Peter Elliott – pictured beating talented runners such as Rob Harrison, David Moorcroft and the great John Walker in 1982 – believes the four-minute 'barrier' is still a time for young runners to aspire to... but shouldn't be the end of their ambitions.

much more rarely. For him: "The simple answer is four minutes should certainly no longer be regarded as a sign of international class – more probably you would need to think in terms of 3:52 for the mile, or the equivalent of 3:34 for 1500 metres, as being at that top level.

"When I wrote a book about the four-minute mile to celebrate the 50th anniversary of Roger Bannister achieving that feat I asked Steve Ovett how he rated four-minute miles in the 21st century, and he was adamant that one of the problems of British miling in the era after Coe-Cram-Ovett from the 1990s onwards was that four minutes was still being thought of as something to aim at, and once it was achieved the athlete concerned could feel that he had 'arrived'. Any such illusions should have been totally destroyed by an achievement in a different event entirely in 1997. A Kenyan named Daniel Komen ran the first mile of a two mile race in 3:59.2 and the second mile in 3:59.4."

Phillips may be right when it comes to top class, but race organiser Fraser Moat is convinced his organisation has a valuable role to play, and that the difference between a mile and 1500 metres can often catch good runners out.

"The mile is 1609 metres, and what's surprising is just how difficult the final 109 metres is... and how long it takes world class athletes to complete the extra distance. One might have though that if an athlete can run 3:44 for 1500 metres, he could easily run 3:59 for the mile. Not true – in fact the conversion is more like 3:41 unless the runner is a very strong 5000/10,000 type.

"I have been organising races for the British Milers' Club (BMC) since 1993. It was founded in 1963 by the late Frank Horwill 'to raise British middle distance running to world supremacy'. We put on a national race programme to help athletes run fast times and set personal bests. In the 1970s our races were frequently used by Steve Ovett and Sebastian Coe, and in the 1980s by Kelly Holmes, as part of their racing programmes.

"Sadly not many mile races are run in the UK these days – this is because all leagues, national and international championships from the youngest age groups hold races over 1500 metres rather than the mile, and an athlete's first priority is naturally to set qualifying times to assist with their selection for their chosen event. The BMC, in conjunction with Oxford University, has an annual mile meeting at Oxford, but that it is about it.

"The last sub-four minute mile I organised was at Oxford in 2004, in the presence of Sir Roger Bannister, to commemorate his 50th anniversary. Craig Mottram of Australia won that day in 3:56.64, and a 21-year-old Mo Farah placed second in 4:00.07. As you can see, even future double Olympic champions can't break four minutes at will. In fact Mo has only broken four minutes for the mile on four occasions, his best being in a BMC race at Crystal Palace in 2005 where he ran 3:56.49.

"It would definitely be a meeting promoter's dream to get Mo to run a mile in 2014."

But that's again a story of facts and figures and statistics... and for the athletes themselves the mile race is so much more, and the word 'race' should never be lost according to Coghlan.

"I was brought up as a racer, I wanted to win... and the thought was that the times would follow. It certainly wasn't the other way around. As I progressed times got faster, and yes, sometimes they became important, but always for me the position, the winning, was most important," said Coghlan.

Yorkshireman Peter Elliott is another of those world class runners from the UK who often gets forgotten in

Daniel Komen has impressed in 1500 metres races in recent years, but still no one has broken Hicham El Guerrouj's best.

LEFT: El Guerrouj of Morocco has taken titles and records, currently holding all four 'mile' bests indoors and out.

BELOW: Four minute mile... How about two in a row? Daniel Komen of Kenya ran a two-mile race in which the first half was completed in 3:59.2 and the second half in 3:59.4.

the glitz and rose-tinted recollection of the 1970s, 80s and early 90s. Never one to break the world mile record, he did hold the world indoor 1500 metres record for a year-and-a-day from February 1990, and for him the mile will always be special, along with the times and efforts of those who went before him.

"Because of the history that goes before it, especially with British milers, the race still draws attention."

Elliott, 51, was always appreciative of the history of the mile, even in his younger days as a junior runner growing up in Rawmarsh, Rotherham.

"In my late teens I read up on stuff and got out books on the great milers," he said. "You are very much aware of that tradition. Iffley Road in Oxford – I've been down to the track there a number of times – and of course the Emsley Carr Mile.

"I was also aware of Derek Ibbotson, how he was actually the first to run the four-minute mile... but Roger Bannister ran it under four minutes. So the exploits of all those guys those were very interesting to me and I have met Derek many times over the years."

As a youngster Elliott started out in cross-country, but graduated to the track, and quickly became aware of those two dominant personalities of the time. "As a 17-year-old I was glued to the telly watching Coe and Ovett do battle in Moscow, that spurred me on."

And as he got older and started competing more seriously, being part of the scene couldn't fail to hone Elliott's competitiveness.

"There were a lot of us around at the time and it was like anything, success breeds success. If it was the UK Championships or AAA Championships, or even for myself as a 16-year-old racing Seb Coe in the Yorkshire Championships, there were always quality fields about and young lads wanted to run 800 and 1500 metres. To break the four-minute mile was a target, and the first time you do it, it is a significant barrier because you join an exclusive club." ➤

ABOVE & ABOVE RIGHT: In 1999 David Moorcroft, then chief executive of UK Athletics, congratulated the winner of the Under 17 Boys CGU British Grand Prix at Crystal Palace. That runner, Mo Farah, has gone on to claim Olympic and World medals at 5000 and 10,000 metres.

Elliott, controversially selected for the British Olympic team in 1988 ahead of Coe, still believes the four-minute mile is something that good club athletes should aspire to.

"In all honesty, I used to run a four-minute mile in training. But it was still a four-minute mile.

"You go to John Walker who was the first man to run 100 sub four-minute miles, and there is that thing about joining the 'Sub-Four Club'. So for any youngster, if they're knocking on the door, it is a magical barrier to break, and still is."

However, Elliott says it should be a springboard for a runner with ambitions, not an end in itself.

Steve Cram still holds the British mile record – 3.46.32 set in 1985 – so does that prove not as many people are running the distance competitively or that UK athletes nowadays aren't as good?

Elliott said: "You have to say Steve Cram was a very talented athlete, and that current British record was at one time the world record. We don't have as many athletes coming through as we did in those days. I think for the younger runners these days, because of the history of the event, the expectations that are placed on their shoulders in enormous.

"Is the talent there? Yes, I'm sure it is."

And for Bob Phillips, the subject will always hold fascination... and plenty of research as he looks at new projects surrounding the quest for the four-minute mile.

"I'm currently researching the numerous stories of a mile having been run in four minutes long before Bannister did so in 1954. There is even reasonably well documented evidence of a man names James Parrot running four minutes for a mile on roads through London in 1780.

"Jack Lovelock is supposed to have run a mile in 3:52.8 in training in the mid-1930s, while a very capable British miler named Ken Wood claimed that he ran 3:59.2 in a time trial a few weeks before Bannister broke through the legendary barrier. Wood might well have done so. He actually ran an official 3:59.3 three years later. None of these stories, or others like them, will ever be proved one way or another – which, of course, makes them all the more interesting."

Does Sir Roger Bannister hold a place in history? Of course, his was a fantastic achievement and numerous great athletes of the time tried and failed, repeatedly, to duck under four minutes, on cinder tracks, with a wide variety of training techniques, with strict amateur regulations which seemed to repeatedly exclude men who could, or should, get there. Haegg and Andersson, if they had been able to progress their times in the late 1940s without being banned, must surely have been able to... but of course, they didn't. It's as pointless an argument to make as the 'who would win in the boxing ring, Joe Louis or Mike Tyson?'... and those types of debate keep pundits going for hours.

> *"I used to run a four-minute mile in training. For any youngster, if they're knocking on the door it is a magical barrier to break."*

Bannister's race went down in history, and rightly so, but in the cold light of 60 years' hindsight, Phillips is one of those who is convinced it should have been done earlier.

"The disruption of the war years put paid to the chances of others. I was in correspondence a few years ago with an American, Walter Mehl, who won the national 1500 metres title in 1940, and he told me that he felt sure that but for the war he or another of his rivals in the USA would eventually have broken four minutes for the mile. Haegg had actually set a World record of 3:43.0 for 1500 metres in 1944, which had been equalled by two other athletes in 1947 and 1952, and this was – as near as makes no odds – the equivalent to four minutes for the mile."

But that's speculation... and great fun too. Bannister IS the man in the history books, and Hicham El Guerrouj is the man in current possession.

Has the mile reached its limit? Probably not, Bannister himself predicted 3:30 was possible, but what is undeniable is that El Guerrouj has taken the sport to a remarkable level, and the quality of his record, 15-year-old as it is, cannot be disputed if only for the fact he also holds the much more often-run 1500 metres record, and that's been in place for 16 years.

The final word here goes to the eloquent Eamonn Coghlan, a man who witnessed first-hand some of the great races of the late 20th century, some of the great records, who held the indoor version of the mile best, and whose son John has now joined him in the 'sub-four club'.

"Sir Roger Bannister was the first to do what many had thought impossible, he was the first to climb that sporting Everest. It's remembered with a real fondness, and those guys from that era are remembered too... and always will be. People like John Walker, Steve Ovett, Jim Ryun, Filbert Bayi, Michel Jazy and Derek Ibbottson. There was a romanticism to the distance and the era

"You need the speed of a sprinter and the stamina and strength of the 10,000 metre runner. You have to have the strength and the kick. The mile runner is the thoroughbred of the track." ∎

ABOVE: In 2004 a men's one mile race was held at Iffley Road in Oxford. Sir Roger Bannister was on hand to greet winner winner Craig Mottram, whose winning time was 3:56.64.

Statistically speaking

TIME	ATHLETE	COUNTRY	DATE
4:12¾	Walter George	UK	Aug 23, 1886
IAAF era			
4:14.4	John Paul Jones	USA	May 31, 1913
4:12.6	Norman Taber	USA	July 16, 1915
4:10.4	Paavo Nurmi	Finland	Aug 23, 1923
4:09.2	Jules Ladoumegue	France	Oct 4, 1931
4:07.6	Jack Lovelock	New Zealand	July 15, 1933
4:06.8	Glenn Cunningham	USA	June 16, 1934
4:06.4	Sydney Wooderson	UK	Aug 28, 1937
4:06.2	Gunder Haegg	Sweden	July 1, 1942
4:06.2	Arne Andersson	Sweden	July 10, 1942
4:04.6	Gunder Haegg	Sweden	Sept 4, 1942
4:02.6	Arne Andersson	Sweden	July 1, 1943
4:01.6	Arne Andersson	Sweden	July 18, 1944
4:01.4	Gunder Haegg	Sweden	July 17, 1945
3:59.4	Roger Bannister	UK	May 6, 1954
3:58.0	John Landy	Australia	June 21, 1954
3:57.2	Derek Ibbotson	UK	July 19, 1957
3:54.5	Herb Elliott	Australia	Aug 6, 1958
3:54.4	Peter Snell	New Zealand	Jan 27, 1962
3:54.1	Peter Snell	New Zealand	Nov 17, 1964
3:53.6	Michel Jazy	France	June 9, 1965
3:51.3	Jim Ryun	USA	July 17, 1966
3:51.1	Jim Ryun	USA	June 23, 1967
3:51.0	Filbert Bayi	Tanzania	May 17, 1975
3:49.4	John Walker	New Zealand	Aug 12, 1975
3:49.0	Sebastian Coe	UK	July 17, 1979
3:48.8	Steve Ovett	UK	July 1, 1980
3:48.53	Sebastian Coe	UK	Aug 19, 1981
3:48.40	Steve Ovett	UK	Aug 26, 1981
3:47.33	Sebastian Coe	UK	Aug 28, 1981
3:46.32	Steve Cram	UK	July 27, 1985
3:44.39	Noureddine Morceli	Algeria	Sept 5, 1993
3:43.13	Hicham El Guerrouj	Morocco	July 7, 1999

Athletics is undoubtably one of the great sports for keeping and quoting statistics. Competitors will be running for personal bests, which could be season bests, age group records, national records, all-comers' records, games records or world records.

When it comes to the mile we're comparing split times and schedules, so it's easy to be quickly baffled and overrun by numbers, facts and figures.

The Sub-4 Register is compiled by Bob Phillips and always make fascinating reading. It was initiated by the late Bob Sparks on behalf of the National Union of Track Statisticians (NUTS) of Great Britain, and was continued by Ian R Smith, and now Bob Phillips, the editor of the quarterly journal of the NUTS, *Track Stats*.

Along with some of the all-time lists, over the next few pages we include just a few of those fantastic facts, and all-time records… at least, at time of writing…

LEFT: Michel Jazy had a devastating turn of pace and held the world record for just over a year in the mid-Sixties.

FATHERS AND SONS...
BY AVERAGE

- **1st** Kip Keino 3:53.1, Martin Keino 3:52.33 (Kenya) = 3:52.71
- **2nd** Matt Centrowitz 3:54.94, Matthew Centrowitz 3:53.92 i (USA) = 3:54.43
- **3rd** Eamonn Coghlan 3:49.78 i, John Coghlan 3:59.52 i (Ireland) = 3:54.77
- **4th** Sam Bair 3:56.7, Sam Bair 3:59.72 i (USA) = 3:58.21
- **5th** Barry Brown 3:58.8, Darren Brown 3:58.85 (USA) = 3:58.83

FAR LEFT, LEFT & ABOVE RIGHT: Kip Keino never held the world record, but he and son Martin have both broken four minutes.

ABOVE: John Coghlan became the latest son to join the Sub-4 Register.

NATION-BY-NATION
...THE TOP 10

1st USA 416; **2nd** UK 189; **3rd** Kenya 134; **4th** South Africa 54; **5th** Australia 52; **6th** Canada 44; **=7th** Ireland, New Zealand 37; **9th** Germany (including East and West) 33; **10th** Morocco 31.

By late 2013, there were just over 1300 athletes who had been registered as running under four minutes for the mile, and as Sub-4 Register author Bob Phillips points out, there are now 17 sets of brothers (including five sets of twins), plus five sets of fathers and sons who have broken four minutes – the most recent addition to this family tradition being John Coghlan, son of Irish former world indoor mile record holder Eamonn – one of those who pushed Filbert Bayi to his record in 1975.

Coghlan senior told the author: "John made me very proud when he went under the mark. It came out of the blue really and I've never put any pressure on him to live up to anything I ever did. He's his own man, and for him to achieve on his terms is fantastic.

"In the case of John, athletics – and indeed his other passion, drumming – has helped take a shy lad with dyslexia and given him so much confidence. But if at any stage he hadn't wanted to do it, if he'd said no, then that would have been no problem. He has surpassed all my expectations, he's 25 now, he has a new coach – I was his coach – but now it has liberated him... and me too!

"He has a passion for athletics and will get stronger over the next two or three years."

Almost 60%t of the 1300-plus athletes listed have not (yet) bettered their first sub-four performance… ➤

WOMEN'S WORLD MILE RECORD SINCE DIANE LEATHER'S FIRST SUB-FIVE MILE

TIME	ATHLETE	COUNTRY	DATE
4:59.6	Diane Leather	UK	May 29, 1954
4:50.8	Diane Leather	UK	May 24, 1955
4:45.0	Diane Leather	UK	Sept 21, 1955
4:41.4	Marise Chamberlain	New Zealand	Dec 8, 1962
4:39.2	Anne Rosemary Smith	UK	May 13, 1967
IAAF era			
4:37.0	Anne Rosemary Smith	UK	June 3, 1967
4:36.8	Maria Gommers	Netherlands	June 14, 1969
4:35.3	Ellen Tittel	West Germany	Aug 20, 1971
4:29.5	Paola Pigni	Italy	Aug 8, 1973
4:23.8	Natalia Marasescu	Romania	May 21, 1977
4:22.1	Natalia Marasescu	Romania	Jan 27, 1979
4:21.7	Mary Decker	USA	Jan 26, 1980
4:20.89	Lyudmila Veselkova	USSR	Sept 12, 1981
4:18.08	Mary Decker-Tabb	USA	July 9, 1982
4:17.44	Maricica Puica	Romania	Sept 9, 1982
4:16.71	Mary Decker-Slaney	USA	Aug 21, 1985
4:15.61	Paula Ivan	Romania	July 10, 1989
4:12.56	Svetlana Masterkova	Russia	Aug 14, 1996

BROTHERS... BY AVERAGE

1st Cornelius Chirchir 3:50.40, William Chirchir 3:47.94 (Kenya) = 3:49.17

2nd Noureddine Morceli 3:44.39, Abderrahmane Morceli 3:54.63 (Algeria) = 3:49.51

3rd Robert Cheseret 3:59.23 i (Kenya), Bernard Lagat 3:47.28 (USA) = 3:53.26

4th Charles Cheruiyot 3:55.41, Kipkoech Cheruiyot (Kenya) 3:52.39 = 3:53.90 (twins)

5th Nick Willis 3:50.66, Steve Willis 3:58.15 i (New Zealand) = 3:54.40

6th Elliott Heath 3:57.91, Garrett Heath 3:53.15 (USA) = 3:54.76

7th Jack Buckner 3:51.57, Tom Buckner 3:58.87 (UK) = 3:55.52

8th Ian Stewart 3:57.3, Peter Stewart 3:55.3 (UK) = 3:56.3

9th Arne Kvalheim 3:56.4, Knut Kvalheim 3:56.2 (Norway) = 3:56.3

10th John Jefferson 3:57.85 i, Sean Jefferson 3:56.44 (USA) = 3:57.14 (twins)

i = indoor

ABOVE RIGHT: The names may be confusing, but Bernard Lagat (pictured) and his brother Robert Cheseret are on the Sub-4 Register, Lagat being a star performer on the US indoor circuit.

LEFT & RIGHT: The Chirchir brothers William (left) and Cornelius (right) are, on average, the fastest siblings to have run sub-four minute miles.

BELOW: One man who never had the chance to make the Sub-4 Register was Ivo van Damme (103). The Olympic silver medal winner was killed just months after the 1976 games in Montreal.

MISSING OUT

Only two of the Olympic 1500 metres medallists since 1956 have not been sub-four milers: Klaus Richtzenhain (East Germany) and Ivo van Damme (Belgium), the silver-medallists of 1956 and 1976 respectively. In the case of van Damme it was because his career was tragically cut short when he died in a car accident shortly after the 1976 Montreal Olympics, aged just 22.

MILE FALLS OUT OF FAVOUR:

As Register editor Bob Phillips points out, there are far fewer sub-four milers than should be the case, mainly because there are many more races at 1500 metres, and numerous 1500 metres runners have never competed over one mile. He cites 2010 as an example, during which 209 athletes ran 3:40.90 or faster for 1500 metres, whereas only 55 men achieved the equivalent time at one mile of 3:58.41.

Two dozen nations have not produced a sub-four miler but have national records for 1500 metres of 3:42.22 or faster.